"Olivia's beautiful new book is a must-have resource for anyone living a gluten-free life. This book easily helps you navigate the changes that eating gluten-free requires by offering both thorough guidance and delectable recipes."
—Gretchen Brown, R.D., author of *Fast & Simple Gluten-Free*

"Olivia Dupin takes you from diagnosis to dinner and beyond with information and mouthwatering recipes everyone can use and enjoy."
—Beth Hillson, author of *Gluten-Free Makeovers* and food editor of *Living Without*

"Olivia has written the over-the-top, go-to guide for gluten-free living. Not only does it arm you with naturally g-free recipes for meals you already know and love, but it also teaches you practical tips for steering clear of the gluten pitfalls of everyday life."
—Jennifer Iserloh, founder of Skinny Chef Culinary Ventures

"This easy-to-follow book is full of invaluable information and amazingly delicious recipes. If you or anyone in your life eats gluten-free, you need to have Olivia's book!"
—Michael Repole, chairman of Pirate's Booty® snacks

The Complete Guide to

NATURALLY GLUTEN-FREE FOODS

Your Starter Manual to Going G-Free the Easy, No-Fuss Way

Olivia Dupin

Includes 100 Simply Delicious Recipes!

FAIR WINDS
P R E S S

First published in the USA in 2013 by
Fair Winds Press, a member of
Quayside Publishing Group
100 Cummings Center
Suite 406-L
Beverly, MA 01915-6101
www.fairwindspress.com

17 16 15 14 13   2 3 4 5

ISBN: 978-1-59233-528-2

Digital edition published in 2013
eISBN-13: 978-1-61058-623-8

Library of Congress Cataloging-in-Publication Data

Dupin, Olivia.
  The complete guide to naturally gluten-free foods : your starter manual to going g-free the easy, no-fuss
way-includes 100 simply delicious recipes! / Olivia Dupin.
      p. cm.
  ISBN 978-1-59233-528-2 (pbk.)
  1. Gluten-free diet–Recipes. 2. Food allergy–Diet therapy. I. Title.
  RM237.86.D87 2013
  641.3–dc23
                        2012023484

Book and Cover Design by Kathie Alexander
All photography by Theresa Raffetto (www.theresaraffetto.com) except as follows:
  Martin Poole/Getty Images, cover image appearing on right; Shutterstock, pages 33; 40; 57; 65.
Food Styling by Matt Vohr for Halley Resources
Prop Styling by Penelope Bouklas

Printed and bound in China

The information in this book is for educational purposes only. It is not intended to replace the advice
of a physician or medical practitioner. Please see your health care provider before beginning any new
health program.

DEDICATION

When I have a big moment approaching,
I do this thing where I call on all of my friends
and family for support. I gather up their words
of encouragement and love, and I feel like
I can do anything. This book is for them;
thank you for lifting me up, every day.

CONTENTS

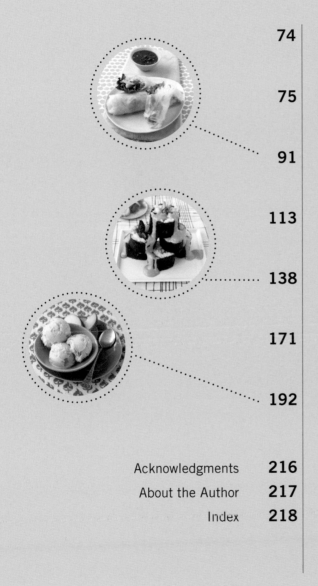

INTRODUCTION

My love affair with food began when I was a little girl. I loved to eat, and soon learned that I loved to cook. Never one to play with dolls, I wore out my Easy-Bake Oven in no time, and before long I'd graduated to the full-size range in my mother's kitchen. Instead of letting the babysitter cater to me when she came over, I would make her scrambled eggs for breakfast. So it didn't surprise anyone when, at the age of eight, I announced that I wanted to be a chef.

When I was a senior in high school, I was accepted to the acclaimed Culinary Institute of America. I tore open the letter, and I cried in the kitchen with my grandma Ginny. It was a dream come true, and I felt so lucky! That fall, I walked around campus like I was at Disneyland. I soaked it all in, and a few short years later, I was out in the world, living my dream working as a private chef to the rich and famous in New York City.

Fast-forward to a few years after that; I was working for a family on the Upper West Side, but I was struggling. I was always exhausted and always getting sick. One day, I was chatting with the personal assistant for the family and I opened up about how sick I had been. For ten years, I told her, I had been suffering with fainting spells, extreme fatigue, brain fog, years of missed periods, and low iron. I had seen several hematologists, but the treatment was always the same. They would hook me up to an IV of iron, where I would sit for about 45 minutes every week. This helped somewhat with the fatigue and fainting, but still, no one could tell me why I was so sick. I was frustrated and scared.

After hearing how much I was struggling, the assistant decided to make a call for me and got me in to see a great doctor she thought might be able to help. He had a hunch, did a few tests, and a couple weeks later, I found out that I had celiac disease. I couldn't believe I finally had a diagnosis. On one hand, I was really upset that no other doctor had caught my condition sooner, but at the same time, I was relieved to finally know why I was so sick. Gluten was the culprit all along, but somehow it had never occurred to me that my symptoms could be related to the foods I was eating.

I was so lucky that I didn't need surgery or expensive medications and treatments to get better, but my first reaction was still panic. What would I eat? How would I cook for my clients? I gathered with a few friends and said goodbye to gluten with a farewell feast consisting of pasta, pizza, garlic bread, and cake—an exercise I don't recommend. I stumbled out of the restaurant that night foggy-headed and a little regretful but ready to start fresh. It really was a new beginning.

I've learned a lot along the way, and today I'm thriving, healthy, and happier than ever. As a chef, food is a huge part of my life. I will not tell you that I never feel tempted or inconvenienced, but I will tell you that I eat delicious, nutritious foods that make me happy and feel good, and so do my clients. I throw gorgeous gluten-free dinner parties for my family and friends who never feel like they are eating "special diet food." The best way I've found to cook nutritiously and deliciously gluten-free is to focus on naturally g-free foods instead of trying to make substitutions for foods like breads and pasta.

I want to help you continue your love affair with food, just as I have. I know how emotional and personal food can be. We have traditions, special occasions, and memories marked and centered around the table. It can be difficult to adjust to a gluten-free lifestyle, learn to cook differently, order at a restaurant differently, and resist old friends like takeout pizza and office birthday cake.

Whether you are one of the growing number of celiac patients, have a wheat allergy or gluten sensitivity, or simply just feel better when you omit gluten from your diet, living a gluten-free lifestyle doesn't have to be stressful or expensive. We'll talk about everything you need to know to get you on the right track simply and effectively. We will focus on the foods you *can* eat, practical tips for stocking a gluten-free pantry (even if you cohabitate with gluten eaters!), easy guidelines for dining out, and really easy, yummy recipes you can put together in no time. Even if you've never cooked before, you can make gourmet dishes like steak with red wine sauce, sinfully tender pulled pork, and creamy, dreamy butterscotch pudding, so you'll never feel like you're missing out on anything. And because all of the recipes in this book use only naturally gluten-free ingredients that you are already familiar with and can find in your regular grocery store—forget those tiny $12 bags of flour, elaborate substitutions, and mediocre results—you'll quickly discover that this is the most practical approach to a gluten free diet around.

Are you ready to begin the journey to better health with me? Let's get started!

PART 1

LIVING GLUTEN-FREE

all about GOING GLUTEN-FREE

Let's start by discussing the basics of what going gluten-free means, and how it can benefit you. We'll take you step-by-step through the process of getting a diagnosis for your symptoms and adjusting to a gluten-free lifestyle.

WHAT IS A GLUTEN-FREE DIET?

A gluten-free diet is one that eliminates virtually all forms of wheat, barley, and rye. It's as simple as that. These foods contain a protein called gluten, which gives breads and pastries their elasticity, chewiness, and bounce. The gluten in these foods also contains a component called gliadin, which is the culprit in a vast array of health issues for millions of people around the globe, which we'll talk more about below.

The most common gluten-containing foods include bread, beer, pizza, pasta, pretzels, crackers, cakes, cookies, muffins, pancakes, doughnuts, and almost all other baked goods. Additionally, gluten is contained in lots of foods you wouldn't suspect, including many packaged and convenience foods. Some chicken stock, licorice, canned frosting, and even corn chips, for instance, can contain wheat, barley, or rye ingredients, so reading labels is extremely important. Even foods that don't contain gluten can be contaminated by coming into contact with equipment that processes these foods (oats are a big one). Check out chapter 3 for an extensive list of the foods you can have, as well as a list of unexpected places you may find trouble.

Navigating a gluten-filled world might seem tricky at first, but it will eventually become second nature to you. There are a lot of adjustments that those on a gluten-free diet will have to make, but you can still eat out and enjoy social functions involving food. Still, your best defense against hidden gluten will be cooking at home, where you can keep track of exactly what goes into the foods you eat and vigilantly prevent cross-contamination. If the kitchen is uncharted territory for you, don't despair. I've laid out all of the basics you need to cook at home and make all of the recipes in this book, and there's even a how-to guide for reading a recipe. By using only ingredients you and your family are already acquainted with, you'll be making gluten-free meals suitable for you and the gluten-gluttons in your life.

WHO CAN BENEFIT FROM EATING GLUTEN-FREE?

The obvious candidates for a gluten-free diet are people who have been diagnosed with celiac disease; however, this is not the only condition that can benefit from a strict gluten-free diet.

Those with Autoimmune Conditions

Some people have an autoimmune reaction to gluten. During an autoimmune reaction, the body mistakes its own tissue as a foreign invader and attacks itself. Gluten-related autoimmune diseases include the following:

■ **CELIAC DISEASE (CD):** Celiac (sometimes spelled coeliac) disease is an inflammatory autoimmune disease triggered by ingesting gluten that causes damage to the small intestine. In a healthy person, hairlike projections in the intestine called villi absorb nutrients into the body. A person with celiac disease, however, experiences an autoimmune reaction to gluten that results in villous atrophy, in which the body's autoimmune response attacks the villi and they become damaged. After extended exposure to gluten, the villi become so matted and flat that they can no longer effectively absorb nutrients from the foods you eat. At this point, the patient has developed celiac disease.

The most commonly known symptom of celiac disease is steatorrhea, a form of diarrhea, or greasy, pale, foul-smelling stools. But only about a third of celiac patients experience this symptom. Other symptoms of CD can range from digestive issues like severe abdominal pain, vomiting, bloating, and gas, to brain fog, delayed growth in children, vitamin deficiencies and anemia, inability to gain weight, tooth decay, missed periods, infertility in women, and low bone density. Some people experience no physical symptoms of the disease until it has progressed considerably. CD with no apparent symptoms is known as silent celiac disease.

One in 133 people in the United States, or about 3 million people, are thought to have CD, and these numbers will continue to increase. The genes DQ2 and DQ8 have been identified as markers for CD. Having these genes doesn't mean that you will definitely get CD, but you can. You have a very slim chance of developing CD if you do not have the DQ2 or DQ8 gene. Have an aunt, an uncle, or a cousin who has been diagnosed? Then you have a 1 in 39 chance of having it as well. If you have a parent, child, or sibling with celiac disease, the odds are 1 in 22 that you have it, too.

Because celiac disease causes malnutrition by interfering with the complete absorption of vitamins, minerals, and nutrients, a gluten-free diet can improve companion diseases and symptoms, including osteoporosis, infertility, and severe and chronic anemia, like I suffered from before I was diagnosed with CD.

The only treatment for CD is a strict, permanent gluten-free diet. With time, a person with celiac disease can be expected to make a full recovery.

■ **DERMATITIS HERPETIFORMIS (DH):** Dermatitis herpetiformis is an intensely itchy skin rash with characteristic red bumps or fluid-filled blisters. The rash most often appears on the buttocks, knees, and elbows but can also appear on the back of the neck, in the scalp, along the hairline, on the groin, or even on the face. DH is not caused by skin contact with gluten, but it is an autoimmune response to ingesting gluten. DH is almost always a symptom of untreated celiac disease.

Dermatitis herpetiformis is diagnosed with a simple skin biopsy. The itching can be treated with medication, but getting rid of DH completely requires eliminating gluten from your diet.

■ **GLUTEN ATAXIA:** Little is known about the condition gluten ataxia. Ataxia is characterized by damage to the cerebellum, which causes mental confusion and disorientation, and disorders in fine movement, balance, and posture.

If you're experiencing any of these neurological symptoms and your doctor can't find the source, they may be related to an autoimmune reaction to gluten and you may have gluten ataxia.

Damage to your brain is permanent and cumulative, because these cells do not regenerate, but an extremely strict gluten-free diet has been shown to stop gluten ataxia from progressing. Physical and occupational therapy may help restore some functionality.

■ **OTHER AUTOIMMUNE DISEASES:** The autoimmune aspect of celiac disease suggests a link to other autoimmune diseases, such as rheumatoid arthritis, lupus, thyroid disease, and type 1 diabetes. It's very important to be tested for celiac disease if you have any of these conditions because people with other autoimmune conditions seem to have an increased likelihood of having CD. You can see an extensive list of associated autoimmune conditions on the chart of Gluten-Related Symptoms and Associated Conditions on page 26.

Those with Gluten Sensitivity (GS)

There are cases where a person experiences symptoms from eating gluten but there is no allergic or autoimmune reaction. These people do not have celiac disease or a wheat allergy. In these cases, the body experiences an immune reaction to gliadin and creates antibodies in the small intestine. This is known as gluten sensitivity or gluten intolerance. It differs from CD because the body does not attack the villi in the small intestine. In these cases, people may experience physical symptoms very similar to those associated with celiac disease, but are more likely to have nondigestive symptoms, including bone or joint pain, muscle cramps, weight loss, and fatigue. It is believed that GS may affect more than six times as many people as CD does.

You may be diagnosed with gluten sensitivity if you experience a reaction to eating gluten but celiac disease and wheat allergies have both been ruled out. For those with GS, a gluten-free diet can make them feel better and greatly improve their health and quality of life.

Those with Wheat Allergies

Wheat allergies differ from CD and GS because those with wheat allergies do not experience an autoimmune response to gliadin found in wheat, barley, and rye. Rather, a person with a wheat allergy can react to any of at least twenty-seven components of wheat, generating allergy-causing antibodies. A person with a wheat allergy experiences symptoms that may include abdominal cramps and diarrhea, nausea and vomiting, hives, headaches and migraines, swelling, trouble breathing, tiredness, and lethargy. It's even possible to have a wheat allergy at the same time as celiac disease or gluten sensitivity. Skin tests or blood tests may be used to diagnose wheat allergies.

People with wheat allergies can avoid an allergic reaction by eliminating wheat, but they don't need to avoid barley or rye. However, some find that a gluten-free diet works best for their lifestyle.

Those Looking to Live More Healthfully

You may not have any of the conditions that require eliminating gluten from your diet. Maybe you've chosen a gluten-free diet in solidarity with someone who has been recently diagnosed with celiac disease or one of the other conditions we've discussed. You've opened yourself up to a new world of delicious, nutritious, and wonderful food choices and are showing your support for someone you love on his or her journey to better health. That's love, baby! Good for you!

Or maybe you're moved toward a gluten-free diet because you just feel better on it. Some claim that it is beneficial for weight loss, and this may or may not be so depending on the changes you make. If you eliminate gluten-containing breads, pastas, and pastries and replace them pound for pound with gluten-free varieties, for instance, your chances of weight loss are slim. Often, more sugar or fat is added to gluten-free alternatives to achieve a desirable consistency, texture, and taste, making them higher in fat and calories than the standard. But, if by eliminating gluten-containing foods like breads, pastas, and pastries you turn to more natural gluten-free alternatives like whole fruits and vegetables and alternative grains like quinoa, then you will be making healthy changes to your diet that may indeed lead to weight loss. The key to weight loss, of course, is to burn more calories than you consume, and there is no miracle diet for that, not even g-free.

Aside from the weight loss aspect, a gluten-free diet can force you to expand your food horizons. It can make you more conscious of the foods you eat and the choices you make each and every time you munch. Maybe you will begin to cook at home more and eat out less. You can discover some new foods you love and replace some of your carb-heavy meals with more plant-based choices. Suddenly your plate is full of color instead of tan, bland carbs, and you're getting more nutrients and variety in your diet than ever before. If you are interested in seeing what a gluten-free diet can do for you, I encourage you to give it a try. A balanced gluten-free diet can be good for anyone!

GETTING DIAGNOSED

It took me ten years (and lots of different doctors) from the onset of my symptoms to finally get a diagnosis, and during that time I got sicker, more frustrated, and less and less hopeful that anyone would ever figure out what was wrong with me. I was pale, weak, and exhausted, and I would faint if I stood in one spot for too long, making lines at the mall or going to a concert risky business.

My doctors knew that I had very low iron, and my blood work showed that I was having some sort of autoimmune response that they could not pinpoint the cause of, but all anyone ever did was treat my symptoms (anemia), not explore where they might stem from. I spent years scared that I had some terrible illness that no one had discovered. I'd spend hours on the Web putting my symptoms into those medical websites and reading about all of the terrifying diseases I convinced myself I may have. Celiac disease was not even on my radar, and it wasn't on my doctors' either. When I pushed for answers, doctors would give me a vague diagnosis like "some people just don't absorb iron the way they should, and you are one of them." I was even told by one of my doctors that I was not a priority because he was dealing with patients who were "really sick." No doctor should ever make you feel unimportant or make you feel like your condition is in your head. You know your own body, and you know when something isn't right. If you think you have an issue with gluten but haven't yet gotten a firm diagnosis, I encourage you to keep persevering.

I'm a strong believer that we need to advocate for our own health as best we can. Finding the right doctor can take time. Sometimes you need to meet with several before you find one you feel completely comfortable with and trust. For some people, a friendly disposition and good bedside manner is really important to making them comfortable. For others, if they feel like they trust and respect their doctor, they are okay if his or her bedside manner leaves something to be desired. If you don't feel completely comfortable with your doctor, it's okay to shop around. I've always had the best luck by asking for a recommendation from a friend or family member. Ask people whose opinion you value. You can also find a specialist in your area through Internet searches, online forums, or your insurance company directory.

GET TESTED!

There is still a lot we don't know about these conditions, so symptoms are still often misdiagnosed or left unexplained. Millions of CD and GS sufferers are undiagnosed. If you're wondering whether you may have CD, GS, or any of the other conditions we've discussed, you are ahead of the game! It's very important to insist on getting tested.

Do your research and if you have questions for your doctor, ask them and keep asking until you understand the answers. According to the University of Chicago Celiac Disease Center, the average symptomatic person takes four years to get diagnosed with celiac disease! As awareness of CD, GS, and other gluten-related illnesses increases, this shocking figure will surely decrease, but in the meantime, it's important that you understand the testing process and ask your doctor for the tests you feel you need so that you don't have to suffer.

The chart on the next page illustrates the conditions we've discussed and the tests used to diagnose them. We'll discuss it in more detail next.

Between 30 and 40 percent of the population in the United States has the DQ2 or DQ8 genes that predispose you to celiac disease. It's still unclear whether you have CD from birth or whether it develops later in life after exposure to gluten, but if you have CD, damage to intestinal villi can manifest at any point from infancy to late adulthood. Because celiac is a progressive disease, you want to catch it before the damage to your intestinal villi is very serious. The sooner your disease is diagnosed, the less damage your body will incur and the faster you will fully recover.

Evidence also shows that the longer you have gluten antibodies running through your veins, the higher the chances of developing another separate autoimmune disease. There is evidence that some autoimmune diseases are associated with untreated CD or GS (see the Gluten-Related Symptoms and Associated Conditions chart on page XX). This is a potentially very serious complication because while you can recover from celiac disease or gluten sensitivity simply by removing gluten from your diet, these other diseases associated with CD or GS do not respond to eliminating gluten.

It's important to note that until you have been tested, you should be eating gluten. I know this may sound absurd, especially if you feel it's making you sick, but in order for diagnostic tests to be accurate, you need to be regularly consuming gluten. If you aren't, your body stops producing the antibodies that the tests look for and it heals itself. This can make tests come back as a false negative for CD or gluten sensitivity.

Diagnosis of Gluten-Related Disorders

				AUTOIMMUNE			NON-AUTOIMMUNE	
				Celiac Disease (CD)	Dermatitis Herpetiformis (DH)	Gluten Ataxia[2] (GA)	Gluten Sensitivity (GS)	Wheat Allergy (WA)
				CD symptoms: diarrhea, malnutrition, brain fog, etc...	Skin manifestation of CD (blistering skin rash)	Ataxia and possible CD symptoms	CD symptoms but no villous atrophy	Respiratory, skin, anaphylactic responses
TEST[1]								
DNA Test			DQ2 or DQ8	Positive	Positive	80% test positive	50% test positive	N/A
DNA Test			DQ1	N/A	N/A	20% test positive	N/A	N/A
Stool Test	Gluten immune reaction	CD or GS	AGA	Positive	Positive	Positive	Positive	N/A
Blood Tests	Gluten immune reaction	CD or GS	AGA	Positive	Positive	Positive	Positive	N/A
Blood Tests	CD-specific blood tests (Any positive test indicates CD antibodies in the blood)	Newest test	DGP	Positive	Positive	Can be pos.	Negative	N/A
Blood Tests		Most common >95% specific	tTG-IgA	Positive	Positive	Can be pos.	Negative	N/A
Blood Tests		Most specific, less sensitive	EMA-IgA	Positive	Positive	Can be pos.	Negative	N/A
Blood Tests	Wheat allergy	Allergy	IgE	N/A	N/A	N/A	Negative	Positive
Intestinal Biopsy				Positive	Can be pos.	Can be pos.	Negative	N/A
Skin Tests		Biopsy	IgA	N/A	Positive	N/A	N/A	N/A
Skin Tests		Skin prick	IgE	N/A	N/A	N/A	N/A	Positive

TEST KEY[1]	
DQ genes	DQ2 or DQ8 genes are found in 98% of celiacs. DQ1 is associated with Gluten Ataxia
Total IgA	IgA Total Immunoglobulin A serum level
AGA	Anti-gliadin Antibody (IgA and IgG)
DGP (aka dAGA)	Deaminated Gliadin Peptide Antibodies (IgA & IgG)
tTg	Tissue Transglutaminase Antibody (tTg-IgA) (or tTg-IgG if you have an IgA deficiency)
EMA	Endomysial Antibody, (IgA only, not useful if you have an IgA deficiency)
IgE	Immunoglobulin E is a type of antibody associated with allergic reactions

[2] Current antibody blood tests for CD antibodies are not sufficiently advanced to reliably diagnose Gluten Ataxia. Current tTG tests for instance, do not test for the tTG6 variant of the antibody. It is recommended that ataxia patients with any anti-gluten antibodies should go on strict GF diet.

TESTING FOR CELIAC DISEASE

The first step to diagnosing CD is to get a panel of blood tests for the antibodies specific to CD. The antibodies you are going to be screened for are anti-tissue transglutaminase (tTG), anti-endomysial antibodies (EMA), and anti-deamidated gliadin peptides (DGP or dAGA).

If you test positive for any of these antibodies, the next step is an endoscopic biopsy. The purpose of the biopsy is to collect actual samples of the lining of the upper part of your small intestine to check whether your intestinal villi are damaged. This is currently the only foolproof way to confirm a CD diagnosis.

Getting a Biopsy

For the biopsy, you will be sedated or put under full anesthesia. An endoscope, a lighted optical instrument with a camera attached, is then threaded down your throat into your stomach and then past the opening of your stomach so that your doctor can observe (on the video monitor) the condition of your duodenum, or the upper part of your small intestine. The doctor then inserts a long flexible biopsy instrument through a small channel in the endoscope and takes several tiny tissue samples of the intestinal lining of the duodenum.

These tissue samples are then sent to a lab, where a pathologist determines the health of each sample. He or she assesses the state of the villi, the small fingerlike projections in your small intestine, as well as other characteristics of celiac disease, such as an increased number of white blood cells.

Assessing the Biopsy Results

The amount or stage of the damage revealed in your biopsy is categorized on a scale called the Marsh Classification. It indicates various levels of damage to your intestine.

- A score of 0 indicates no sign of inflammation or damage, or a negative result for celiac disease.
- A score of 1 or 2 indicates mild inflammation or damage, indicating that the patient may have celiac disease but it has not progressed sufficiently or it is being treated with a gluten-free diet.
- A score of 3 (3a, mild atrophy; 3b, marked atrophy; or 3c, complete atrophy) indicates that you are positive for celiac disease with villous atrophy at various stages of severity.

The chart below illustrates the different stages of CD and GS and where symptoms and test results that correspond with these stages fall. The terms *silent celiac disease* and *silent gluten sensitivity* refer to those who have CD or GS but do not have the physical symptoms associated with the conditions. *Potential* or *latent CD* refers to CD that has not progressed to the point where villi damage is present.

Stages of Celiac Disease and Gluten Sensitivity

		DQ2 or DQ8 Genes	Celiac-Specific Antibodies	dAGA Antibodies	Intestinal Villi Damage	Physical symptoms
CD	Active Untreated CD	Positive	Positive	Positive	Positive	Positive
	Silent CD	Positive	Positive	Positive	Positive	Negative
	Latent or Potential CD	Positive	Positive	Positive	Negative	Negative
	Controlled with GF Diet	Positive	Negative	Negative	Negative	Negative
GS	Active Untreated GS	Can be positive	Negative	Positive	Negative	Positive
	Silent GS	Can be positive	Negative	Positive	Negative	Negative
	Controlled with GF Diet	Can be positive	Negative	Negative	Negative	Negative

Treatment

The only way to treat CD is with total avoidance of gluten in your food (which this book will guide you through). There are no medications that can prevent an autoimmune or immune reaction to gluten.

Passing Down CD

As we discussed, a child whose mother or father has CD has a 1 in 22 chance of developing the disease. If you or a family member has CD and you are worried your child or children may have it, you can have them tested for the genes associated with the disease. With the DNA test, you can rule out the possibility that your child will ever develop the disease. If the DNA test is negative, your child doesn't have the gene for celiac disease, and therefore it's extremely improbable that he will develop CD. If the genetic test is positive, your child does have a chance of developing the disease. If this is the case, your doctor will likely recommend antibody blood testing every two to three years to see whether your child has developed any autoimmune reaction to gluten. If you see symptoms or suspect your child has celiac disease prior to your next appointment, however, don't wait. Ask for the test right away.

If you've found out your child has the gene, can you do anything to prevent passing CD on to your child? Some believe that how and when you introduce gluten into your child's diet may help reduce the likelihood of your child developing CD. Doctors seem to disagree, however, on exactly when the best time is to introduce gluten-containing foods to babies. Some say gluten should be introduced no earlier or later than six to seven months to minimize the likelihood of developing CD or sensitivities. Others say to avoid all major allergens (milk, egg, fish, shellfish, tree nuts, peanuts, soybeans, wheat, and gluten) completely in the first year. Still others say you should only introduce gluten-containing foods to your child while simultaneously breastfeeding, as evidence supports that breastfeeding benefits your baby's immune system and passes along important antibodies and enzymes your child needs.

If this sounds confusing, you aren't alone. The truth? There may not be anything you can do to prevent your child from developing CD if he or she has the gene. Consult your child's doctor about the best plan of action and introduce gluten-containing foods when it feels right for you.

TESTING FOR A WHEAT ALLERGY

If you have a wheat allergy, you will most likely experience symptoms within a few minutes or hours after exposure to wheat. The reactions can range from very mild headaches to a rare but more severe anaphylactic reaction. If you suspect you have a wheat allergy, your doctor will utilize blood and skin tests to make a diagnosis.

A blood test is the first test your doctor will perform to test for wheat allergies. This test measures your immune system's response to wheat by measuring the amount of allergy-causing immunoglobulin E (IgE) antibodies in your bloodstream.

An allergy skin test may also be performed. During the test, the skin on your arm or back is pricked and extracts from wheat proteins are introduced onto the skin's surface. After a few minutes, the skin is checked for signs of a reaction to the wheat extracts. If you don't react, the test is negative. If your skin develops bumps or a red, itchy rash, your test is positive.

If these tests are inconclusive for wheat allergies, an oral food challenge may be utilized for diagnosis. By eliminating wheat and monitoring how your body reacts, your doctor may conclude that you have a wheat allergy.

Treatment

A wheat allergy is treated by eliminating your exposure to wheat. Depending on your allergy, this may include eliminating wheat from your diet as well as your exposure to wheat through contact with your skin or inhalation of flour particles in the air.

CELIAC DISEASE AND INFERTILITY

Infertility is an often missed symptom of undiagnosed CD. Women with undiagnosed CD can begin their periods later, have lapses in time with no period (amenorrhea), and experience menopause sooner.

Iron, folate, zinc, B vitamins, and calcium are among the nutrients essential for a healthy pregnancy. Damage to intestinal villi can make proper absorption of these nutrients impossible for someone with untreated CD. Deficiency in these nutrients can lead to miscarriage, preterm delivery, low birth weight, neural tube defects, and preeclampsia.

If you are having trouble having a baby and think undiagnosed CD may be associated with your troubles, talk to your doctor right away about getting tested. It has been shown that within a year of following a strict gluten-free diet, chances of conceiving improve for many women.

TESTING FOR GLUTEN SENSITIVITY

The term gluten sensitivity (GS) can seem very ambiguous. In June 2011, a preliminary definition of the term gluten sensitivity was written at the 11th International Celiac Disease Symposium in Oslo, Norway. The symposium concluded that gluten sensitivity is essentially a diagnosis of exclusion. This means that you have symptoms similar to CD after consuming gluten, but have negative diagnoses of both celiac disease and wheat allergy.

There are several other key elements in determining whether you have GS:

1. You have a positive reaction to the AGA (anti-gliadin antibody) test, meaning that your body is reacting to gliadin.
2. You have a negative blood test to transglutaminase IgA (tTg-IgA) or the endomysial antibodies (EMA), tests that are specific to CD only.
3. You have a biopsy that shows no atrophy of the villi.
4. (Optional) You have a negative DNA test for the DQ2 and DQ8 genes that are specific to CD. You are extremely unlikely to have CD if you do not possess either one of these genes (but you still may have gluten sensitivity).

Treatment

Gluten sensitivity is thought to affect an even larger portion of the general population than celiac disease. Many of the symptoms of gluten sensitivity are indistinguishable from those of CD. For a comprehensive comparative list of the different symptoms, complications, and possible associated diseases and conditions, refer to the Gluten-Related Symptoms and Associated Conditions chart on page 26.

The treatment for gluten sensitivity is the same as it is for celiac disease: total avoidance of gluten in your diet.

ALTERNATE TESTING OPTIONS

There are a few other options for testing for celiac disease and gluten sensitivity that don't involve blood testing, but they do come with added costs that may not be covered and/or supported by your doctor and insurance company.

Home DNA Kit

Some independent labs, such as Kimball Genetics, offer at-home genetic test kits for celiac disease. They retail for about $300. You don't need to have blood drawn; you simply swab the inside of your cheek with the supplied swab and send the sample to the lab. Within days, you or your doctor will receive your DNA results along with an analysis. Although these labs will most likely be out of network for your insurance company, it should be possible for you to receive partial reimbursement if prescribed by your doctor. You should contact the lab for assistance in ordering and billing so that you and your doctor have the proper paperwork.

Stool Testing

Research is currently being done to develop more sensitive tests that can diagnose celiac disease before the villi are damaged. These anti-gluten antibody tests may also detect gluten sensitivity earlier than the standard blood tests.

Developed by Kenneth Fine, M.D., founder of EnteroLab in Dallas, Texas, the tests are purported to be significantly more sensitive than current blood tests because they test the level of antibodies in the stool (feces), rather than the blood. This method is based on research conducted by an English research group, which discovered that they could detect IgA antibodies to gliadin much earlier in the development of celiac disease if they measured these antibodies in the intestinal fluid, where the body first encounters gliadin. Dr. Fine claims that the number of people who test positive to anti-gliadin and anti-tissue transglutaminase IgA antibodies through these stool tests is about three times higher than the number detected using blood tests. He also reports that the fecal anti-gliadin IgA test is positive in 100 percent of untreated (gluten-eating) celiac disease patients.

It is important to note that although these tests are affordable—the basic Gluten Sensitivity Stool Test (Fecal Anti-Gliadin IgA) costs about $100—they are still new and are not likely to be accepted by your doctor. That said, they can be a very valuable alternative tool in detecting gluten sensitivity (GS) and silent or early-stage celiac disease that does not present intestinal villi damage. Also, the higher sensitivity of these tests means that they may be the only way to confirm GS or celiac disease if you have been on a gluten-free diet for an extended period of time (i.e., more than six months). They are also an alternative for patients who dislike blood tests or who choose not to go back to eating gluten for testing purposes.

GLUTEN-RELATED SYMPTOMS

The chart below compares and contrasts the symptoms and conditions associated with celiac disease, gluten sensitivity, and wheat allergies.

BODY'S RESPONSE							
AUTOIMMUNE			NON-AUTOIMMUNE				
Celic Disease (CD)	Dermatitis Herpetiformis (DH)	Gluten Ataxia	Gluten Sensitivity (GS)	Wheat Allergy (WA)	Symptoms and Conditions	Occurence	Remarks
x	x	x	x		Severe fatigue, weakness, dizziness, fainting	Common	
x	x				Skin lesions (dermatitis herpetiformis [DH])	Common	Small, very itchy blisters that erupt on the elbows, knees, buttocks, back, or scalp
					Gastrointestinal Symptoms		
x	x	x	x	x	Abdominal pain	Common	
x	x	x	x		Bloating	Common	
x	x	x	x	x	Diarrhea or loose stools	Common	
x	x	x	x		Steatorrhea (greasy, foul-smelling, pale stool)	Common	
x	x	x	x		Irritable bowel syndrome (IBS) symptoms	Common	
x	x	x	x		Constipation	Common	
x	x	x	x		Acid Reflux	Common	
x	x	x	x	x	Nausea, vomitting	Common	
					Brain Functions		
x	x	x	x	x	Poor concentration, brain fog	Common	See anemia, depression, and ADHD
x	x	x	x	x	Memory problems	Common	See anemia, depression, and ADHD
x	x	x	x	x	Depression	Common	
x	x	x	x	x	Migraines	Common	
x	x	x	x	x	Attention deficit hyperactivity disorder (ADHD)	Common	

(cont'd)

| BODY'S RESPONSE | | | | | | | |
| AUTOIMMUNE | | | NON-AUTOIMMUNE | | | | |
Celic Disease (CD)	Dermatitis Herpetiformis (DH)	Gluten Ataxia	Gluten Sensitivity (GS)	Wheat Allergy (WA)	Symptoms and Conditions	Occurence	Remarks
					NEUROLOGICAL AND PSYCHIATRIC ASSOCIATIONS		
x		x			Ataxia (balance disorders)	Common	Should always be tested for CD
x	x	x			Peripheral neuropathy	Common	Also associated with diabetes
x	x	x	x		Schizophrenia	Possible	
x	x	x			Epileptic seizures	Possible	
x	x	x			Fibromyalgia	Possible	
x	x	x			Autism (ASD)	Possible	
					MALABSORPTION/ MALNUTRITION- RELATED COMPLICATIONS		
x	x	x			Osteoporosis or osteopenia	Common	Results from malabsorption of calcium, vitamin D, and magnesium. Also associated with an overactive thyroid.
x	x	x			Difficulty in becoming pregnant	Possible	
x	x	x			Miscarriage	Possible	
x	x	x			Neural tube birth defects (e.g., spina bifida)	Possible	Folic acid and B12 deficiency during pregnancy
x	x	x			Low birth weight	Possible	
x	x	x			Short stature (failure to grow normally)	Possible	
x	x	x			Failure to thrive	Possible	
					Anemia from iron, folate, or B12 deficiency		
x	x	x			Severe fatigue, weakness, dizziness, fainting	Common	
					Vitamin deficiencies		
x	x	x			B vitamins	Common	
x	x	x			Folate (folic acid)	Common	
x	x	x			Fat-soluble vitamins (D, A and E)	Common	Associated with steatorrhea

BODY'S RESPONSE							
AUTOIMMUNE			NON-AUTOIMMUNE				
Celic Disease (CD)	Dermatitis Herpetiformis (DH)	Gluten Ataxia	Gluten Sensitivity (GS)	Wheat Allergy (WA)	Symptoms and Conditions	Occurence	Remarks
					MALABSORPTION/ MALNUTRITION-RELATED COMPLICATIONS		
					Mineral deficiencies		
x	x	x			Iron deficiency	Common	Leads to Anemia
x	x	x			Calcium deficiency	Common	Leads to Osteoporosis
x	x	x			Magnesium and zinc deficiency	Common	Leads to Osteoporosis
					Lactose intolerance	Common	
x	x	x			Decreased calcium levels	Common	Damage to the villi stops lactose production
					OTHER PHYSICAL SYMPTOMS		
x	x	x	x		Bone and joint pain	Common	Joint pain and inflammation and migraine headaches
x	x	x			Weight loss	Common	
x	x	x			Mouth ulcers	Common	
x	x	x			Changes in dental enamel	Common	
x	x	x			Bleeding or bruising tendency	Common	
					ALLERGIC REACTIONS		
				x	Baker's asthma (from breathing in flour)	Common	
				x	Wheat dependent exercise-induced anaphylaxis (WDEIA)	Common	
				x	Aspirin-induced anaphylaxis	Common	
				x	Hay Fever (allergic rhinitis)	Common	
				x	Swelling and itching of mouth and throat	Common	
				x	Hives or rash	Common	
				x	Contact urticaria	Common	
				x	Eczema (atopic dermetitis)	Common	
				x	Itchy watery eyes	Common	
				x	Difficulty breathing	Common	
				x	Sacroillitis	Common	
				x	Angioederna (swelling)	Common	

(cont'd)

| BODY'S RESPONSE | | | | | | | |
| AUTOIMMUNE | | | NON-AUTOIMMUNE | | | | |
Celic Disease (CD)	Dermatitis Herpetiformis (DH)	Gluten Ataxia	Gluten Sensitivity (GS)	Wheat Allergy (WA)	Symptoms and Conditions	Occurence	Remarks
					AUTOIMMUNE-RELATED COMPLICATIONS		Occurs three to ten times more frequently than normal
x	x	x			Type 1 diabetes	Common	Should always be tested for CD
x	x	x			Thyroid disease (Graves or Hashimoto's disease)	Common	Should always be tested for CD
x	x	x			Autoimmune liver diseases	Common	
x	x	x			Celiac hepatitis	Common	
x	x	x			Microscopic colitis	Common	
x	x	x			Peripheral neuropathy	Common	
x	x	x			Addison's disease	Possible	
x	x	x			Sjögren's syndrome	Possible	
x	x	x			Rheumatoid arthritis	Possible	
x	x	x			Psoriasis	Possible	
x	x	x			Eczema	Possible	
x	x	x			Alopecia areata	Possible	
x	x	x			Crohn's disease	Possible	
x	x	x			Lupus	Possible	
x	x	x			Cardiomyopathy	Possible	
x	x	x			Cerebral vasculitis	Possible	
					CANCER		
x	x	x			Non-Hodgkin's lymphoma	Possible	
x	x	x			Enteropathy-associated T-cell lymphoma (EATL)	Possible	
x	x	x			Adenocarcinoma of the small intestine	Possible	
x	x	x			Thyroid cancer	Possible	

ADJUSTING TO A NEW LIFE AND A NEW YOU

So, you officially have a condition that requires that you avoid gluten permanently. If you struggled for a long time with your symptoms, having a diagnosis is probably a huge relief. Although you don't need surgery or medications to get better (a great thing!), there is no quick fix, either. The changes in your diet that you make now will carry through for the rest of your life. The good news is, once you get on a track with a strictly gluten-free diet, you should begin to feel better and better each day.

A lot of people joyfully give up gluten and never look back, so happy to just feel better. But what if you were shocked, angry, or frustrated when you learned that your diet would have to change permanently? I feel for you. Finding out that you have to change the way you cook and eat is a game-changer for a chef or anyone who loves food, hates change, or doesn't like to be told what to do. Sound like you? It's okay to feel freaked out or panicked at first. Food is a really emotionally charged topic for most people. Social events center around food. Meals are the epicenter of family togetherness. We look to food to celebrate the good times, and to comfort us when we are sick or sad. So the last thing I'm going to promise you is that the instant you go gluten-free, life will be like skipping through a field of daffodils. But as your health returns (or appears for the first time for some people), you will find that the obstacles are nothing in the face of health and happiness.

The great news is that now you are in control of your health and getting well is up to you, but if you are in fact feeling sad, resentful, or scared about the changes you are going to have to make, then you need to deal with that first and foremost. Have you ever been through a traumatic breakup? Consider this your breakup with gluten. You need time to mourn, so give yourself a few days to mope over it. When you are done feeling good and sorry for yourself and have accepted that eating gluten-free is for the best, then remember this: Gluten (that deadbeat!) was only hurting you. Now you can move on, find foods that love you for you, and make yourself happy inside and out!

Check out support groups in your area if you feel like you need a little extra TLC. It might even help to see a dietician who can counsel you on your diet and help you make the changes that will work for you.

Cheating

I'd be doing you a disservice if I told you I've never cheated and knowingly ate gluten. Yes, you've read correctly. I've cheated on my gluten-free diet. You probably will, too, either accidentally or with reckless abandon. It's important to address the fact that cheats happen and you need to consider what it means for you.

Before I say anything else, know that my stance is that any cheating, ever, is an absolute no-no. But we're humans, we make mistakes, and we hopefully learn from them. I consider myself to be a really average twenty-something woman, and as a result, I find that my feelings, struggles, and opinions aren't all that unique. I share my experience with you in the spirit of full disclosure, so you know you aren't alone if you've felt the way I have.

Growing up, I had two working parents and a working stepparent. That meant that by a certain age, if I was sick from school, I stayed home alone. Once my celiac symptoms sprung up in high school, this was pretty darn often. When I was too sick or just too plain exhausted from being so anemic to go to school, my mom would slap ten bucks on the counter as she headed off to work, and tell me to order myself some lunch. My favorite was Chinese takeout—it was my comfort food. It's pretty funny that all those years I was sick and struggling unknowingly with celiac disease, I was turning to gluten-laden sesame chicken and fried rice to "comfort" myself.

Well, old habits die hard, and in times when I need a little comfort, I still turn to food. Although my palate has expanded since then, Chinese takeout will always feel like comfort food to me. In really low moments, I've reached for the phone and ordered up some General Tso's chicken and steamed dumplings. At the time, it seemed like a good idea. But, in the end, the greasy takeout isn't ever as good as I remember it being, and I am left feeling guilty and sick. One thing I have found is that once you go gluten-free, if you do eat gluten, the physical symptoms you experience are even more intense than they were before you stopped. I never had gastrointestinal symptoms from eating gluten, but the heavy-headed brain fog and fatigue I experienced came back with a vengeance. Every time I have cheated, I've regretted it, so now it's easier to make the right decision in the face of temptation.

There are tons of other justifications for cheating on a gluten-free diet. Here are a few you may have already wrestled with:

- "I forgot and ate something I should not have." This might happen in the beginning of your diet. It's forgivable. We're creatures of habit and we sometimes eat without even thinking. With time, you'll learn to think about every single thing you put in your body and slip-ups like this will become less likely.

- "There was nothing else for me to eat." Avoid this one by always, always having a snack on hand. I carry snacks like the Honey Nut Trail Mix Bars on page 110 with me at all times because you never know where you might wind up in your adventures throughout the day. Always have a backup plan in the form of gluten-free sustenance just in case.

- "Gluten-free foods don't taste good." I can't completely disagree with this one. Some packaged gluten-free foods taste, well, *bad*, and if you look at these items as the benchmark of the gluten-free diet, you will certainly get discouraged. Happily, as the gluten-free diet becomes more and more mainstream, the amount of quality gluten-free products has increased as well. But there are thousands of naturally delicious gluten-free foods you can have. Flip to the encyclopedia on page 62 if you need more convincing, or check out the 100 beautiful and extremely delicious recipes (if I do say so myself) in the second half of this book. Naturally gluten-free foods are delicious, can be made with familiar ingredients you already know and love, and are easy to make.

- "I don't feel sick when I eat gluten." If you are one of the people who have celiac disease but don't experience any painful manifestations of the disease, consider yourself already blessed. But rest assured, if you continue to eat a diet that contains gluten, then you will continue to harm your body. Think of smokers who smoke cigarettes. In the short term, they may not see any adverse effects to their health. It is certainly not painful to smoke a cigarette, but in the long run they are doing serious damage to their lungs, esophagus, and overall health. It is the same with gluten for you. Continue to eat gluten and you will cause serious damage to your body. Check out the sidebar "What If I Eat Gluten Anyway?" on page 34 for more on that.

- "It's hard to eat out gluten-free." Yes, yes it is. This isn't always the case, but it really can be at first. Going out should be relaxing and fun, but sometimes it just feels like people have no idea what you are talking about when you say, "I'm gluten-free." It can be frustrating, but you do have options at a restaurant, and usually plenty of them, which is why I've laid out exactly how to handle g-free dining on page 47.

If you do cheat, all is not lost. Don't think that because you've cheated there is no point in following a gluten-free diet any longer. You need to get back on the wagon and do it right away. You deserve it, and your health depends on it.

Dealing with Cravings

Studies indicate—as if we didn't already know—that cravings are generally in your head. Before my diagnosis, I never liked pizza very much (french fries have always been my guilty carb of choice!), but now that I know I can't have it, walking past Patsy's Pizza in New York City sends a pang of longing through me. Isn't that the way it always goes? We don't like to be told no, do we? When the little devil appears on your shoulder telling you it's okay to cheat just this once, what should you do? Let me tell you what helps me best:

1. **De-stress.** Because cravings seem to appear most often when we are really stressed out, try, at least in the beginning of your gluten-free journey, to keep your stress level to a minimum. Planning your day and your downtime will keep you feeling in control.

2. **Give in to temptation in other ways.** Craving something chocolaty? Instead of chocolate chip cookies from the office vending machine, have a small chocolate bar. You'll get your fix and stay on track if you choose gluten-free foods that make you feel like you've indulged instead of sacrificed.

3. **Plan meals ahead.** Knowing what you are going to eat throughout the day can help keep you from feeling anxious about mealtimes. Have a plan and stick to it.

It might seem really hard at first to overcome cravings. In the beginning, you might feel hungry all the time and be preoccupied with eating. This is normal. A gluten-free diet is a lifestyle change, and that can be a really big deal. With time, practice, and patience, you will get a handle on your cravings and discover new and delicious foods that won't send you off track.

WHAT IF I EAT GLUTEN ANYWAY?

If you have celiac disease and you eat gluten, you will get sicker. As you know, celiac disease is an autoimmune disorder, and the damage to your body is cumulative. There are countless complications to untreated celiac disease that may not appear for several years.

Because celiac disease affects the absorption of vitamins and minerals in the small intestine, if you continue to eat gluten, your villi do not have the chance to heal, and instead of absorbing vitamins and minerals, your body excretes them through bowel movements. This can cause lots of problems, including malnourishment.

Malnourishment can lead to anemia, or a deficiency of iron, folate, or vitamin B12. Sufferers can become calcium deficient and develop osteopenia and osteoporosis. Children can become underweight and experience stunted growth. Women may experience missed periods, early menopause, and infertility.

Furthermore, production of the enzyme lactase, which aides in the digestion of lactose (found in dairy products), is hindered by damaged villi, and untreated CD can often cause lactose intolerance. (Findings show that with a proper gluten-free diet, lactase production will eventually return and lactose intolerance will resolve itself.)

In addition to these issues, untreated celiac disease has been shown to cause increased risk of gastrointestinal cancers (including intestinal lymphoma), depression, seizures, and other neurological conditions. This neurological damage is irreversible but can be slowed or stopped with a gluten-free diet.

So don't be fooled into thinking that you will be just fine if you eat gluten and have CD—you may not experience these adverse symptoms right away, but eventually they will greatly affect your health. You deserve to be your best self, and that means staying gluten-free for a life of health and happiness.

Recovering from Accidental Gluten Intake

Accidentally ingesting gluten can happen even to the most careful people, especially if you eat out at a restaurant or in someone else's home. Do your best to identify where the slip may have occurred so that you can avoid the mistake again. Retrace your steps, make a list of everything you've eaten in the past day or so, and try to find the culprit. Identifying where the gluten came from will help you become smarter about staying g-free without incident.

For some, accidental gluten ingestion can be an extremely painful ordeal. Some find themselves in bed for days, with severe cramps, bloating, and diarrhea. There are a few things you can do to help alleviate your symptoms, however. First and foremost, don't panic. Accidents happen and you are going to be okay.

You may think inducing vomiting is a good idea, but doctors recommend against this because it's traumatic to the body. Chances are it will not decrease your likelihood of experiencing a reaction anyway.

Over-the-counter remedies used to treat upset stomach and diarrhea, such as Pepto-Bismol, can really help soothe your symptoms. Some people swear by probiotics or digestive enzymes, such as GlutenEase or Gluten Digest, which may help manage the symptoms caused by accidental gluten ingestion. It's recommended that these enzymes be taken as close to the time of gluten ingestion as possible to be most effective. These pills may help some people but should not be considered a cure for celiac disease. They do not make it okay to cheat, and they do not prevent an autoimmune reaction.

I've also heard of lots of home remedies to help with the symptoms, including drinking apple cider vinegar, a spoonful of honey, or even a shot of tequila! I can't vouch for any of these, but you are welcome to look into them if you feel they are a safe option for you.

Ultimately, the most beneficial thing you can do is to make yourself comfortable and ride out the symptoms. Try taking a warm bath, eating mild, easy-to-digest, comforting foods, and getting plenty of rest. In a few days, you will be feeling great again. Most of all, remember that an isolated gluten slip is nothing that will cause irreparable damage, so don't dwell on it. Staying on track day to day is the most valuable thing you can do for your health.

HEALING YOUR BODY

If you have celiac disease, the amount of time it takes to heal your body after going gluten-free depends on how long you went undiagnosed and the extent of the damage to your intestine. The small intestine isn't actually "small" at all—on average, it is about 22 to 23 feet (6.7 to 7 m) long. That's a lot of healing!

How old you were at the time of onset of CD and how long you went undiagnosed will really affect how long it takes to heal. Younger people tend to heal faster, but it all depends on your body and how you respond to a g-free diet. Everyone is different. You may start to feel better as soon as you start the gluten-free diet, or it may take weeks or months. For older patients who have had untreated celiac disease for a long time, healing can take up to two years.

You're going to need follow-up care with your doctor beginning three to six months after diagnosis (see the next section), and if you find that you don't feel well after testing shows that your body is healing, talk to your doctor. You may have some other undiagnosed condition or food allergy that is making you sick.

Also, ask your doctor about recommended supplements or vitamins you can take. For those with celiac disease, your body has not been getting the nutrients it needs, so upping your nutritional intake will help you heal and feel better faster.

Follow-up Care with Your Doctor

Your relationship with your gastroenterologist needs to continue after your CD diagnosis. You should always follow the recommendations of your doctor, but it's generally recommended that you visit for a follow-up three to six months after your diagnosis and again after being on a gluten-free diet for one year. After that, yearly follow-up testing is sufficient. If it's been years since your diagnosis and you haven't received any follow-up care, it's never too late to start. People with celiac disease should see their doctor once a year to ensure they are doing well with their diet and the disease isn't active.

The follow-up tTG-IgA blood test will be the first test your doctor performs. A celiac patient who is following a strict gluten-free diet will have a negative result, meaning that no antibodies are present. Autoimmune conditions, like thyroid disease or type 1 diabetes, however, can throw off the tTG-IgA test results, so AGA (anti-gliadin antibodies) tests may be performed as well. These AGA tests, also check for antibody response to gluten; the results of these tests should be a value as close to zero as possible, which indicates there is no measurable antibody response to gluten.

Follow-up testing can offer huge peace of mind that your gluten-free diet is working and that you are on the road to healing and becoming healthy. If you've been experiencing other physical symptoms and wondering whether they are related to your celiac disease, the tests can help rule out any connection and hopefully help get to the root of those issues, whether celiac related or not.

If you've been anemic, your doctor may also do some blood tests to check on your red blood cell counts. A CBC (complete blood count) will help ensure that your new diet is helping to resolve your anemia by increasing your nutritional absorption.

GLUTEN-FREE KIDS

Maybe you don't have any issues with gluten, but suspect your child might. As with adults, symptoms in children can run the gamut from serious and painful to nonexistent (up to 60 percent of children with CD are asymptomatic). Often, the first physical symptoms may be digestive and stomach upset, including chronic diarrhea or constipation and bloating. Many children are underweight, aren't growing the way they should, or enter puberty late (failure to thrive). Talk to your pediatrician about testing your child for celiac disease if he or she experiences these symptoms.

Explaining a New Diet to a Child

If your child is old enough to recognize that there are going to be some changes to his or her diet, there will probably be questions, and maybe some resistance to those changes. I'm a big believer that we don't really need to dumb it down for kids. They usually appreciate it when you give it to them straight and feel grown-up and responsible if you treat them like the new diet is something they are capable of handling.

If you're sitting your child down to talk about her new diet, chances are she has some idea that there are changes coming because she's been visiting doctors and going through some tests, and has now arrived at a diagnosis (either celiac disease, gluten sensitivity, or wheat allergy, as the case may be). Explain to your child that because of the special way her body works, some foods can make her sick. Explain that the foods she can't have contain something called gluten and that it isn't something she can see or know is there just by looking. If your child is old enough, talk about wheat, barley, and rye being the foods that are on the list of foods she can't have. Mention the foods in your child's diet that will have to change. For example, if your child loves spaghetti, you might mention that the spaghetti she's been eating is not good for her diet any longer, but that she can still have spaghetti if she eats a special kind called gluten-free spaghetti. Focus on the positive and point out all of the favorite and familiar foods your child loves that she can still have. Make sure your child knows how to explain to other adults what her restrictions are for situations when she may be on her own.

Discuss all of the ways that the new diet will help your child feel better by talking about the symptoms your child has that will go away with time on the g-free diet. Some kids will respond right away with lots of questions. If your child has questions, do your best to answer them. You can even search for the answers together in books or online. Some children might not give much of a response at all as they take it all in, and others might get very upset to learn they can no longer eat some of their favorite foods. Give your child some time to process the information you've given her, then revisit the conversation later and answer any questions she may have. The great news is that most kids adjust more quickly and easily than adults do.

Mealtime is an especially great time to discuss these things, and it always helps to make something g-free that your child already knows and loves to remind her that there are still really yummy foods she can eat. Try cooking a new and tasty gluten-free recipe with your child. Getting kids involved with cooking teaches them great things about where food comes from and builds confidence and valuable skills. Best of all, kids are always more willing to try new foods if they've had a hand in preparing them.

Here are a few kid-friendly recipes you might enjoy making together:

- Try the Soft Corn Tortillas on page 176 (you can leave out the chipotle peppers to make them mild). Kids love to help press tortillas in a tortilla press.
- Sushi is a great way to get your kids to eat more veggies and is super fun for them to make! You can find the recipe on page 152.
- Try the Five-Ingredient PB&J Cookies on page 210 for an easy, sweet treat.

Navigating School Lunchtime

Make sure you let your child's teacher know about his or her new dietary restrictions. Food allergies are so much more prevalent with children today that you may find that your child's school does have ways to accommodate a gluten-free diet. If the school has a lunch program, ask if it caters to specific diets and allergies. If it does not, your best bet for ensuring your child eats safe, healthful meals is to send packed lunches.

It's a no-brainer that you can make your child's sandwich on gluten-free whole-grain bread for an easy g-free alternative, but following are some additional ideas for naturally gluten-free lunch and snack options.

■ SANDWICH ALTERNATIVES

- Turkey cheese wraps: Wrap sliced turkey around string cheese sticks for a high-protein portable lunch.
- Chicken skewers: Kids love anything served on a stick! Thread strips of chicken breast onto skewers and bake. Serve with ketchup, honey mustard, or BBQ sauce.
- Rice cake sandwiches: I make these with brown rice cakes to get in some whole grains. They make a great PB&J!
- Tuna or chicken salad wrapped in lettuce leaves: I make these with sweet Bibb lettuce. Kids love the crunch, and the smaller leaves (toward the heart) are the perfect size for little fingers.
- Quesadillas: You can make quesadillas with soft corn tortillas. Fill with cheese or other toppings, then cook in a dry skillet until crispy and the cheese is melted. Cool, slice, and pack!
- Shrimp Summer Rolls (page 104): These can be altered to suit your child's tastes and utilize whatever leftovers you have on hand. Kids love the chewy texture of the rice paper rolls, and because they require no cooking, they are quick and easy to make. Try rolling with shredded chicken, avocado and mango, or ham and cheese.

■ NATURALLY G-FREE PACKABLE SNACKS

- Baby carrots or cucumber slices and hummus (try the Red Pepper Hummus on page 106)
- Dried fruit and nuts
- Edamame
- Fresh whole or sliced fruit (I skewer tiny "kebabs" by threading diced fruit onto toothpicks)
- Hard-boiled eggs
- Homemade granola bars (page 110)
- Low-fat yogurt
- Popcorn (try the Stovetop Cinnamon Kettle Corn on page 112)

■ MY PICKS FOR PACKAGED G-FREE SNACKS

- Baked tortilla chips
- Cinnamon Chex
- Clif Kid Organic Twisted Fruit
- Kozy Shack rice pudding cups
- Pirate's Booty

Navigating Parties

If your child has a gluten restriction, you don't want him to miss out when it's time for a party. Often, at school parties, the birthday child will bring in cupcakes, cookies, or some other goodie on the "no-no" list for your kid. To keep your child from feeling left out, provide his teacher with some of your child's favorite packaged snacks to keep on hand. Cookies, chocolates, and muffins are all good choices. Let your child choose his favorites.

If it is your child's birthday, there are some great options for gluten-free treats he can bring to school. Any of the cakes or cookies in this book would be a great choice, or try one of the following options:

- **Dirt cups:** Top chocolate pudding cups with shaved chocolate "dirt" and gummy worms.
- **Crispy rice squares:** Make sure the crispy rice is labeled gluten-free because this cereal can sometimes contain barley malt. I like to use brown crispy rice for added nutrition. Top with sprinkles to make them really festive.
- **Chocolate fondue:** Kids have an absolute blast getting messy and feasting on fondue (which might make this option better suited for at-home parties). It's great for dipping fruit and marshmallows. Try the Chocolate Peanut Butter Fondue on page 196.

A BALANCED GLUTEN-FREE DIET: GETTING THE PROPER NUTRITION

If you've just been diagnosed with celiac disease, you may find out from your doctor that you are deficient in some vitamins (most often folate, B12, and iron), because damaged villi in the intestine cannot effectively absorb these nutrients. Alternatively, if you are like me, you may have found out about your vitamin deficiency first, and the celiac disease later. You may have (like me) struggled to maintain healthy counts of these vitamins because of the damage done to your body by untreated celiac disease. But by following a strict gluten-free diet, your body will begin to heal and will be able to better absorb these nutrients.

Your doctor may choose to put you on supplements or give you intravenous or intramuscular injections to increase your counts, but as you begin to heal and your body becomes better able to absorb nutrients, natural food sources will be the best way to give your body the vitamins and minerals you need.

Although malabsorption doesn't affect those with gluten sensitivity or wheat allergies, going gluten-free is a big change to your diet, and it's important to ensure that your new diet is a balanced one.

Vitamins and Minerals

Before going gluten-free, one of the most important fortified foods in your diet was probably enriched wheat flour, which is an important source of the vitamins and minerals thiamin, riboflavin, niacin, folic acid (the synthetic form of folate), iron, and calcium. Folic acid in particular is a very important nutrient; it is vital in preventing brain damage in babies caused by neural tube defects, and it is also believed to be helpful in preventing heart attacks, strokes, and colon cancer.

EATING G-FREE WHILE PREGNANT

Pregnancy is a time of cravings and crazy changes in your eating habits. If you have celiac disease, it is important to stick to your gluten-free diet very strictly. If you eat gluten during pregnancy, you put yourself and your baby at risk for deficiencies of essential nutrients during this important developmental period.

If you were accustomed to eating lots of breads, pastas, and foods made with enriched wheat flour before going gluten-free, you may find your new diet lacking in these nutrients. Gluten-free alternatives made with refined (not whole-grain) gluten-free flours are not fortified with vitamins and minerals the way enriched wheat flour is. As a result, it's important that you pay particular attention to consuming enough folic acid, iron, and B12 in other ways to prevent you from developing anemia. You can obtain these nutrients in your diet by:

- Taking a daily multivitamin supplement.
- Consuming gluten-free whole-grain foods. (Look for the Whole Grains Council stamp on the box—aim for at least 51 percent whole grain, ideally 100 percent.)
- Eating a diet naturally rich in these vitamins and minerals (list follows).

■ FOODS HIGH IN IRON

- Beef
- Chicken
- Chicken or beef liver
- Crab
- Edamame
- Halibut
- Legumes (e.g., chickpeas, navy beans, pinto beans, split peas, kidney beans, lentils)
- Molasses
- Oysters
- Pork
- Raisins
- Shrimp
- Spinach
- Tofu
- Tuna
- Turkey

■ FOODS HIGH IN FOLATE

- Asparagus
- Avocado
- Bananas
- Beef liver
- Broccoli
- Cantaloupe
- Corn
- Eggs
- Green peas
- Legumes (e.g., chickpeas, navy beans, pinto beans, split peas, kidney beans, lentils)
- Oranges
- Papaya
- Peanuts
- Romaine lettuce
- Spinach
- Strawberries
- Tomato juice

■ FOODS HIGH IN VITAMIN B12

- Beef liver
- Caviar
- Cheese
- Clams
- Crab
- Lobster
- Octopus
- Salmon
- Sardines

Fiber

Dietary fiber is the indigestible portion of plant foods. It has many health benefits. It keeps you from getting constipated, lowers your risk of diabetes and heart disease, lowers blood cholesterol, and helps regulate blood sugar.

Fiber is commonly divided into two categories: insoluble fiber and soluble fiber. Insoluble fiber doesn't dissolve and passes through the body intact, acting as a broom to sweep material through the digestive tract. Insoluble fiber is particularly beneficial to those suffering from irregular bowel movements or constipation.

Soluble fiber attracts water and forms a gel-like material. It slows digestion and leaves you feeling fuller longer. It can lower your risk of heart disease and lowers blood cholesterol and glucose levels.

The Institute of Medicine of the National Academies recommends that men under age fifty consume at least 38 grams of fiber per day, and men over age fifty consume at least 30 grams. Women under age fifty should consume at least 25 grams per day, and women over age fifty at least 20 grams per day.

To keep your intake up, look for or make baked goods and pastas with high-fiber, whole-grain, gluten-free flours, such as those made from brown rice, quinoa, oats, chickpeas, almonds, or coconut. Those made with refined "white" starches, like white rice or tapioca, are less nutritious.

■ GLUTEN-FREE WHOLE GRAINS

Many people confuse "whole grain" with "whole wheat," but not all whole-grain products contain wheat. The Whole Grains Council explains whole grains like this: "Whole grains or foods made from them contain all the essential parts and naturally occurring nutrients of the entire grain seed. If the grain has been processed (e.g., cracked, crushed, rolled, extruded, and/or cooked), the food product should deliver approximately the same rich balance of nutrients that are found in the original grain seed."

There are also lots of whole grains that are gluten-free and high in fiber. Below is a list of gluten-free whole grains that you may consume whole or in flour form:

- Amaranth
- Brown rice
- Buckwheat
- Corn
- Indian ricegrass (Montina)
- Millet
- Oats (if labeled gluten-free)
- Quinoa
- Sorghum
- Teff
- Wild rice

■ **HIGH-FIBER PRODUCE**

The absolute best way to incorporate more fiber into your diet is with nonstarchy vegetables and fruits. They are generally low in fat and calories and dense with nutrients and phytochemicals, which can help fight cancer. The fruit and vegetables listed below have a very high fiber content:

- Apples
- Avocado
- Bananas
- Berries
- Brussels sprouts
- Carrots
- Collard greens
- Kale
- Kiwi
- Legumes
- Mushrooms
- Orange
- Pears
- Peppers
- Potatoes
- Prunes and other dried fruits
- Pumpkin
- Spinach
- Sweet potatoes

EATING OUT

In the fast-paced world we live in, eating out has become a regular part of many people's routines. Cooking at home is the absolute best way to guarantee that the foods you are eating are safe for you and g-free. But going out to eat with friends, mingling at a cocktail party, and attending a wedding or other special event are parts your life you've probably come to enjoy very much, and you don't want to give them up. Nor should you have to! It's going to take more work than before, especially in the beginning as you learn to get the hang of things, but with time, you'll be able to explain your dietary limitations clearly, ask for what you need graciously, and eat and enjoy safely no matter where you dine.

Ordering at a Restaurant

Ordering gluten-free at a restaurant can be tricky business. After all, there are no labels to read, you can't watch how your food is prepared, and your server has to act as a liaison between you and the person or people who are actually preparing your meal to communicate your special needs.

If you are lucky enough to live in a major city, chances are there are some restaurants in your area that are exclusively gluten-free. These are great options for those who have just been diagnosed because it eases some of the stress of adjusting to this new life. It can be really encouraging to see a full menu that is safe for you to eat, without being tempted by something off-limits or having to wave off the bread basket.

If you don't have exclusively gluten-free restaurants in your area, you still have options. Inquire with your server to see whether they have a g-free menu available. Most restaurants that are health focused (e.g., vegetarian, organic, etc.) cater to special diets and have gluten-free options. These restaurants tend to be more cognizant of how foods are prepared and what goes in them. They are usually a great choice for gluten-free dining. Today, even most chain restaurants are trained and able to cater to almost any dietary restriction. Chains can usually offer you a separate menu or a list of items on their menu that are gluten-free. I've even seen gluten-free items marked with a special symbol on the regular menu.

If a restaurant does not offer a gluten-free menu, that does not mean you can't go there and enjoy a meal safely. First, if circumstances permit, try calling ahead and letting the manager know when you are coming in and that you have a gluten restriction. This will give the staff a chance to prepare for your arrival, do some research if they don't already know about gluten-containing foods, and be ready to accommodate you when you arrive. If you don't have the chance to call ahead or decide to eat out on a whim, keep reading for more tips on how to ensure you get a safe and delicious meal.

■ EMPOWER YOUR SERVER

Tell your server you have special dietary restrictions, that you eat gluten-free, and that you cannot have wheat, barley, or rye ingredients. Ask the server to have the chef make some suggestions from the menu that suit your diet. If you are in the mood for something in particular, let the server know. For instance, when the server comes over to take your drink order, you might say, "I'm on a strict gluten-free diet. I was wondering if you could ask the chef to recommend some items on the menu that are safe for me to eat. I was thinking of starting with one of your salads and I'd like to have fish for my entrée." The server will usually come back with a list of items suggested by the chef that are safe for you to eat, and you can make your decision from there.

■ GUESS AND CHECK

If I have had a chance to scan the menu before a server gets to the table, I can wind up with my heart set on a particular dish before I've had a chance to find out whether it's gluten-free. In these cases, I have already made my best guess that the item is g-free because none of the descriptors on the menu indicate gluten ingredients (e.g., the meat is grilled and topped with salsa, and it's served with roasted potatoes and sautéed veggies).

LOOK IT UP!

The Gluten Intolerance Group (www.gluten.net) offers a restaurant guide where you can search for gluten-free friendly restaurants by ZIP code all over North America.

When this happens, I'll say to the server, "I'm on a strict gluten-free diet. I had my heart set on the grilled skirt steak, but will you check with the chef to ensure that it's gluten-free? If not, I'm open to the chef's recommendations." That gives the server the chance to very quickly find out from the chef whether your order is gluten-free; if it isn't, they can sometimes tweak the dish to make it gluten-free or can recommend similar items you might enjoy.

■ WHEN THE FOOD COMES OUT WRONG

If you order your Caesar salad with no croutons and it comes out with croutons, don't try to be agreeable and just pick them off. Not only is your salad contaminated with gluten that will make you sick, but you also send the message that it's okay that your request for gluten-free items wasn't taken seriously, and that does a disservice to the whole g-free community! Instead, politely inform the server of the mistake, but be sure to mention that you will need a new salad made for you, because just picking off the croutons isn't good enough.

■ WHEN THEY DON'T GET IT

Sometimes, despite your best efforts, the staff doesn't understand exactly what gluten is. As the gluten-free diet becomes more mainstream this is happening less and less, but occasionally you will find an establishment where your server, the manager, and the chef simply don't understand what gluten is and which foods contain it.

I remember ordering seafood risotto once and asking the server to double-check that there were no gluten ingredients in the dish (stock is an ingredient of risotto, and premade stock can often contain wheat). The server came back to me and said, "The chef said you can't have the risotto because it's made of pasta." Confused, I inquired a little further, and he explained to me that rice was a pasta, and that it contained wheat. Of course, rice isn't a pasta; it is a grain and is gluten-free, but the server and the chef didn't know or understand that.

The lesson? When you go out to eat, you cannot assume that the staff members are food and allergy experts who know better than you about what is gluten-free. A lot of the time, the staff members are very knowledgeable, but sometimes they aren't. They can confuse gluten-free with low-carb or other special diets and make mistakes. With time and patience, you will help the staff understand what you can eat safely.

Weddings and Other Catered Events

Weddings are so much fun and can be something to look forward to and enjoyed even if you need to avoid gluten. If you are going to a wedding or other catered event, you should let the bride or host know when you RSVP about any special dietary restrictions you have. This is really easy if the RSVP card comes with a check box for entrée selection. In this case, just write in a little note that you will need a

CHEAT SHEET

An eating out "cheat sheet" can really help spell the do's and don'ts of a g-free diet and help the server and chef at a restaurant understand what you can and can't have. Feel free to make copies of this sheet and take it with you to pass on to your server when you go out to eat.

GLUTEN-FREE RESTRICTIONS

I cannot eat gluten, which means that I cannot have any foods that contain or have come into contact with:

- Barley
- Oats that are not labeled "gluten-free"
- Rye
- Wheat

This includes items such as:

- Bread
- Bulgur
- Durum
- Farro
- Kamut
- Most soy sauces
- Pasta
- Seitan
- Semolina
- Spelt
- Triticale

Please Note

- Tiny amounts of these foods can make me ill, so please use care to avoid cross-contamination by using clean cutting boards, utensils, and equipment.
- Please read labels on any prepared sauces, stocks, or other ingredients that you don't make in-house.
- Foods dusted in flour or bread crumbs will make me sick, and even foods (such as french fries) that are fried in the same oil as breaded items can make me sick.
- I can have other starches, such as: buckwheat, corn, potatoes, quinoa, and rice.

Thank you so much for using care to prepare my meal.

GLUTEN-FREE RESTRICTIONS

I cannot eat gluten, which means that I cannot have any foods that contain or have come into contact with:

- Barley
- Oats that are not labeled "gluten-free"
- Rye
- Wheat

This includes items such as:

- Bread
- Bulgur
- Durum
- Farro
- Kamut
- Most soy sauces
- Pasta
- Seitan
- Semolina
- Spelt
- Triticale

Please Note

- Tiny amounts of these foods can make me ill, so please use care to avoid cross-contamination by using clean cutting boards, utensils, and equipment.
- Please read labels on any prepared sauces, stocks, or other ingredients that you don't make in-house.
- Foods dusted in flour or bread crumbs will make me sick, and even foods (such as french fries) that are fried in the same oil as breaded items can make me sick.
- I can have other starches, such as: buckwheat, corn, potatoes, quinoa, and rice.

Thank you so much for using care to prepare my meal.

GLUTEN-FREE RESTRICTIONS

I cannot eat gluten, which means that I cannot have any foods that contain or have come into contact with:

- Barley
- Oats that are not labeled "gluten-free"
- Rye
- Wheat

This includes items such as:

- Bread
- Bulgur
- Durum
- Farro
- Kamut
- Most soy sauces
- Pasta
- Seitan
- Semolina
- Spelt
- Triticale

Please Note

- Tiny amounts of these foods can make me ill, so please use care to avoid cross-contamination by using clean cutting boards, utensils, and equipment.
- Please read labels on any prepared sauces, stocks, or other ingredients that you don't make in-house.
- Foods dusted in flour or bread crumbs will make me sick, and even foods (such as french fries) that are fried in the same oil as breaded items can make me sick.
- I can have other starches, such as: buckwheat, corn, potatoes, quinoa, and rice.

Thank you so much for using care to prepare my meal.

gluten-free meal and follow up with the bride or groom closer to the wedding date if you find it appropriate.

If the meal is going to be served buffet style, or if you aren't asked to make your entrée selection ahead of time and you don't want to bother the bride or host, you can always call ahead to the venue the week before and talk to a manager so that he or she knows what your needs are. Large venues and caterers are usually well versed in all sorts of special requests and dietary restrictions and can usually handle your request. Just be sure to identify yourself to a member of the staff when you arrive at the venue. You can even slip them a gluten-free cheat sheet for good measure!

Cocktail or Dinner Parties

If you've been invited to a cocktail or dinner party in someone's home, it can feel really uncomfortable to make your special needs known to the host because it's easy to feel like an inconvenience. After all, someone is going through the trouble of cooking and making a special meal for guests, and if you've ever hosted yourself, you know how much work and stress can go into hosting a party in your home.

By the same token, if people have taken the time to plan and cook, then one of their guests arrives and can't eat the food they have prepared, that can be hurtful or embarrassing to the host as well. In a perfect world, you and the host are already acquainted and he or she knows all about your special needs, so a tiny reminder might be all that is necessary. But in some cases you may not even know the host (if you are someone's "plus one," for example), and then what is appropriate?

Because a good guest never arrives to a party empty-handed, I always make and take a gluten-free dish with me. If you can, let the host know ahead of time that you have gluten restrictions, then ask what you can bring.

If you'd rather say nothing about your restrictions, eat before the party in case there aren't many g-free options. That way, you can nibble on gluten-free foods if they happen to be available, but you won't feel starved if the options are slim.

These foods are generally safe at a cocktail party:

- Bacon-wrapped scallops, dates, or shrimp
- Crudités (raw vegetables and dip)
- Deviled eggs
- Fruit or cheese platter
- Nuts
- Plain chips and dips like hummus, salsa, or guacamole
- Shrimp cocktail or raw bar

Use your best judgment and do what feels right and polite for you, but never insist that a host make concessions.

Adjusting to a gluten-free lifestyle takes time, but, the sacrifices you make will be rewarded several times over with good health and wellness!

Chapter 2

the GLUTEN-FREE KITCHEN

By knowing how to read labels on packaged
items, avoid cross-contamination in your
kitchen, and stock the essentials in
your pantry, cooking gluten-free at home
will be safe and simple!

To stock a gluten-free kitchen safely and effectively, you're going to first need to know how to read an ingredient label. Without current labeling standards in place, it can be confusing, but rest-assured we will sort it all out!

DECIPHERING FOOD LABELS

The Food Allergen Labeling and Consumer Protection Act (FALCPA) of 2004 regulates how major food allergens are declared on food labels. The major food allergens are considered milk, eggs, fish, shellfish, tree nuts, peanuts, soybeans, and wheat (note that this list does not include barley or rye. FALCPA requires food manufacturers to label food products that are made with an ingredient that is a major food allergen in one of the two ways shown below.

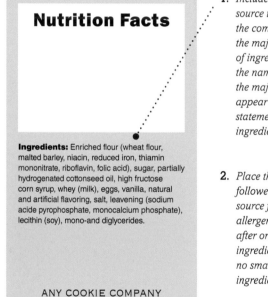

1. *Include the name of the food source in parenthesis following the common or usual name of the major food allergen in the list of ingredients in instances when the name of the food source of the major food allergen does not appear elsewhere in the ingredient statement for another allergenic ingredient.*

- OR -

2. *Place the word "Contains," followed by the name of the food source from which the major food allergen is derived, immediately after or adjacent to the list of ingredients, in a type size that is no smaller than that used for the ingredient list.*

Nutrition Facts

Ingredients: Enriched flour (flour, malted barley, niacin, reduced iron, thiamin mononitrate, riboflavin, folic acid), sugar, partially hydrogenated cottonseed oil, high fructose corn syrup, whey, eggs, vanilla, natural and artificial flavoring, salt, leavening (sodium acid pyrophosphate, monocalcium phosphate), lecithin, mono- and diglycerides.

● **Contains:** Wheat, Milk, Egg, and Soy.

ANY COOKIE COMPANY
COLLEGE PARK, MD 20740

SOURCE: U.S. FOOD AND DRUG ADMINISTRATION, "GUIDANCE FOR INDUSTRY: A FOOD LABELING GUIDE."
WWW.FDA.GOV/FOOD/GUIDANCECOMPLIANCEREGULATORYINFORMATION/GUIDANCEDOCUMENTS/FOODLABELINGNUTRITION/FOODLABELINGGUIDE/UCM064880.HTM.

It is important to note, however, that although manufacturers are required to indicate that a product contains any of the major allergens as an ingredient, they are not currently required to include an advisory statement on the label indicating the possibility of cross-contamination with statements such as, "This product was made in a facility that processes wheat." Some companies include this information voluntarily, but if a label doesn't include it, there are no guarantees that the food product has not been cross-contaminated.

Proposed FDA Rules for G-Free Labeling

The Food and Drug Administration (FDA) is currently in the process of establishing criteria for what qualifies a food to be labeled as gluten-free. Establishing a standard of what is g-free will compel all manufacturers to meet the same requirements and will empower consumers to be informed shoppers.

The proposed definition of the term gluten-free for voluntary use in the labeling of foods would mean that the food does not contain any of the following:

- An ingredient that is a species of wheat, rye, barley, or a crossbred hybrid
- An ingredient derived from these grains and that contains gluten
- An ingredient derived from these grains and that has been processed to remove gluten, if the use of that ingredient results in the presence of 20 or more parts per million (ppm) gluten in the food
- 20 ppm or more gluten. The FDA considers 20 ppm to be the lowest level of gluten that current testing methods can reliably and consistently detect. This tiny amount of gluten is considered safe for consumption by celiacs.

Voluntary Gluten-Free Certification (GFCO)

Certain food companies participate in a voluntary gluten-free certification program by the Gluten-Free Certification Organization (GFCO), a part of the Gluten Intolerance Group. GFCO gluten-free certification requires:

- Periodic gluten testing in the manufacturing facility using GFCO approved testing methods, to meet the minimum GFCO standard of less than 10 ppm gluten in a finished product.
- Periodic plant inspections by a GFCO-contracted auditor.
- Random product testing from end-user shelves by GFCO.

You can find a list of currently certified gluten-free products by GFCO on their website. Products certified by GFCO have this symbol on the package:

Contradictory Information

The label on the right is taken from a box of protein cookies that proudly claims to be gluten-free in three different places on the actual box. For many of us, this would be reassurance enough that the bars are safe to eat. A quick glance at the ingredients confirms that the bars themselves contain no wheat, barley, or rye, but after checking a little more closely, you can see that they are produced in a facility that processes wheat.

Are the bars safe for celiacs to consume? It's hard to tell. Because they are claiming to be gluten-free, the manufacturer may take precautions to ensure that the bars aren't contaminated during production, but is that enough? Without government standards currently in place, they can make this gluten-free claim without testing the bars for less than 20 ppm of gluten, so we cannot know for sure. It's ultimately up to you to decide whether it's a risk you're willing to take (or worth contacting the company over), but do exercise caution when reading and analyzing any product—even those that tout a "gluten-free!" claim.

How Can You Tell by the Label if Your Food Is Gluten-Free?

A definitive answer would be very reassuring, but unfortunately, you can't always tell from the label whether your food is gluten-free. This doesn't mean that you should be paranoid about a can of chickpeas or a gallon of milk. Most single-ingredient foods present nothing to worry about. These types of foods are usually not processed in plants that process gluten and should be no problem.

The most questionable additives are made from wheat (rather than barley or rye) and therefore are required to carry the FDA's allergen advisory, which is helpful. But, because there are no real regulations to confirm whether ingredients were processed in a facility with these allergens, there is still a risk of cross-contamination for some foods. Consuming foods with the Certified Gluten-Free seal or from a company that uses ELISA testing for gluten is currently the best assurance. You can also contact the manufacturer directly if you have questions about a particular product.

Nutrition Facts

Serving Size 1 cookie (40g)

Amount Per Serving

Calories 150	Calories From Fat 50

	% Daily Value*
Total Fat 6g	**7%**
Saturated 3g	**10%**
Trans 0g	
Cholesterol 15mg	**7%**
Sodium 140mg	**6%**
Total Carbs 18g	**6%**
Dietary Fiber 4g	**16%**
Sugars 9g	
Proteins 10g	**20%**
Vitamin A	**0%**
Vitamin C	**40%**
Calcium	**15%**
Iron	**1%**

*Percent Daily Values are based on a 2,000 calorie diet.

Ingredients: Hormone-Free Whey and Milk Protein Concentrates (rBST/rBGH-free), White Chocolate Chips (Sugar, Cocoa Butter, Lecithin, Vanilla), Organic Brown Rice Syrup, Organic Inulin (Blue Agave), Vegetable Glycerin, Macadamia Nuts, Brown Sugar, Organic Coconut Oil, Sunflower Oil, Natural Flavors, Non-GMO Sunflower Lecithin, Baking Soda, Sea Salt, Antioxidant Blend (Green Tea Extract, Vit C [ascorbic acid]), Stevia Leaf Extract (Natural Sweetener), and Xanthan Gum. Non-GMO all natural ingredients.

Contains Milk and Nuts. Manufactured in a Facility that Processes Peanuts, Eggs, Treenuts, Soy and Wheat.

Look carefully at the allergen warning for products that are processed in a facility that processes wheat. This is a sign that there may be cross-contamination.

YOUR BEST BETS FOR SAFE BUYING

Here's what to look for to help determine whether packaged foods are safe for you to eat:

- Look for the Certified Gluten-Free seal from the Gluten-Free Certification Organization.

- Look for products that state they utilize ELISA testing to check for gluten in their products.

- Look for products without any gluten ingredients listed that also have an allergen advisory stating that they are manufactured in a dedicated gluten-free facility, or at least in a facility that does not process wheat.

- Look for oats in the ingredients list. If they are not labeled as "gluten-free oats," they are likely contaminated and the product is not gluten-free.

Some markets, like Trader Joe's, also offer shopping guides that list gluten-free items in their store. Ask around!

NATURALLY GLUTEN-FREE IS BEST

You may have heard that the healthiest way to shop is around the perimeter of the grocery store, where the produce, dairy, and proteins live. This is especially true for anyone avoiding gluten because unprocessed fruits, vegetables, dairy, and meats are all g-free! If deciphering gluten-free items on the shelves feels daunting to you, I encourage you to focus on these foods. They are the healthiest items for any diet, gluten-free or otherwise, and they are the ingredients I focus on in the recipes section of this book.

STOCKING YOUR GLUTEN-FREE PANTRY

Believe it or not, I know as well as anyone how tough it can be to fit cooking into a busy lifestyle. I spend all day preparing beautiful meals for my clients, and honestly, sometimes the idea of cooking at home at the end of the day can be daunting. I know everyone feels that way sometimes, and that is why it is so important to keep your pantry well stocked to make cooking at home easy and enjoyable. Cooking for yourself is the absolute best way to ensure that you are eating gluten-free because you know exactly how your food is prepared and what goes into it. Having the basics on hand will help you avoid a trip to the store every time you set out to cook a meal and will save you time and money.

In keeping with the theme of this book, I'm going to focus on naturally gluten-free basic staples you can find at your regular grocer. It is true that a lot of grocery store chains are now beginning to carry some gluten-free alternatives to items like bread and cereal, which is fantastic. But at my local store, dry spaghetti made with wheat flour costs about $1.25 for 16 ounces (448 g), or just under $0.08 cents per ounce, while gluten-free rice spaghetti costs $3.99 for 12 ounces (336 g), or about $0.33 an ounce. Yes, it's about four times more expensive to use the gluten-free alternative! Similar is true for breads and most other gluten-free replacement foods. Feel free to stock them if you can't live without them, but do remember that there are plenty of naturally gluten-free foods that don't require a substitution, can save you a bundle, and can feed the entire household (gluten-free or not) out of the same pot, simplifying mealtime.

On the next page is a list of my recommended pantry staples. Having items like these always on hand will make shopping easier and mealtime planning a breeze.

Pantry Staples

Apple cider vinegar
Balsamic vinegar
Canned and/or dry beans
Canned tomatoes
Canola oil
Chicken, beef, and/or vegetable
  stock (check the label—don't
  buy any that contain hydrolyzed
  wheat protein)
Chocolate chips
Coconut milk
Cornstarch
Dried fruit
Extra-virgin olive oil
Fish sauce
Honey
Maple syrup
Mirin
Nonstick cooking spray (avoid
  cooking sprays formulated spe-
  cifically for baking, which can
  have wheat flour added)
Nuts
Oats (labeled gluten-free)
Peanut butter and other nut butters
Polenta
Quinoa
Red and white wine
Rice
Sesame oil

Spices

Bay leaves
Black pepper
Cardamom
Cayenne pepper
Chili powder
Cinnamon
Coriander
Crushed red pepper flakes
Cumin, ground
Curry powder or garam masala
Garlic powder
Ginger, ground
Mustard, dry
Nutmeg, whole
Onion powder
Oregano
Paprika
Rosemary
Saffron
Sage
Salt, kosher
Star anise
Tarragon
Thyme
Turmeric
Sugar (granulated, brown, and
  powdered)
Vanilla extract

Refrigerator Staples

Butter or margarine made without
  hydrogenated oils
Carrots
Celery
Cheeses
Dijon mustard

Eggs
Fresh herbs
Heavy cream
Hot sauce
Jams or jellies
Ketchup
Mayonnaise
Milk or dairy milk substitute, such
  as almond or soy milk
Olives
Pickles
Salsa
Tofu

Freezer Staples

Bacon
Boneless skinless chicken breasts
Boneless skinless chicken thighs
Frozen fruit
Frozen vegetables (e.g., mixed
  vegetables, peas, edamame, etc.)
Ice cream
Shrimp

Produce Staples

Apples
Bananas
Garlic
Lemons
Onions
Other fresh fruits
Potatoes
Sweet potatoes
Tomatoes

MAKING YOUR KITCHEN A GLUTEN-FREE ZONE

We've established how important your own kitchen is if you are gluten-free. Keeping it safe isn't difficult, but it does require a little more TLC than it used to. If your entire household will now be gluten-free, you will want to scour labels and get rid of gluten-containing foods and anything that may have become contaminated (such as a jar of peanut butter or any condiments that may have accumulated gluten-containing bread crumbs), then clean all surfaces and cooking equipment very well. You may also want to consider throwing away wooden utensils and cutting boards (these have porous surfaces that may trap and hold gluten-containing particles) and any equipment that cannot be cleaned thoroughly, such as a toaster. If you live with gluten eaters who intend to stay gluten eaters, it may not make sense to rid the house of all gluten-filled foods, but it is important that everything be stored and labeled properly.

HOW TO HANDLE COMMUNAL ITEMS

What about food items that don't contain gluten but can become contaminated during daily use, such as butter, jams, jellies, spreads, and condiments? We've all seen the crumbs left behind after your knife goes back and forth from bread to jar, and those tiny crumbs are enough to make you feel crummy! To avoid getting sick, you have two options for these items. One is to have duplicates of each spread or condiment and clearly label (with colored masking tape, a sticker, or a symbol made with a permanent marker) which one is now intended for gluten-free use and which one is not. Your other option is to replace these items with new, uncontaminated containers, then establish a household rule that no one "double dips" into these jars, but instead portions the item, such as butter, onto their plate with a clean utensil and then spreads the item from their plate to their food. This can take some practice and constant reminding at first, especially for the children in the house. Still, this may be the better solution if your space or budget is limited. If you can find condiments like mayonnaise or mustard in squeeze jars, pick them up! It's an easy way to avoid cross-contamination.

Maybe it's been a while since you cleaned and organized your kitchen. Now is the perfect time! Start in the cabinets and pantries and work your way to the fridge. Pull out everything, and wipe down all surfaces thoroughly to get rid of crumbs and flour particles. Read all food labels carefully, and separate out anything that contains gluten in the ingredients or may be questionable. These items will now be discarded or stored in their own pantry or on shelves below your gluten-free items; the reason behind this is that if you store anything that can potentially contaminate your gluten-free foods above the g-free items, you risk crumbs or food particles falling into or onto gluten-free items. If the gluten-free items are stored on top, this won't happen. If you have the space, however, it will definitely be easiest and most convenient to have separate cabinets or pantries for the g-free and g-filled items. As an additional precaution, you can store gluten-free items in sealed containers or zipper-top bags to prevent any accidental gluten access.

When it comes to kitchen equipment, it's generally accepted that a thorough washing with soap and water will keep cross-contamination of gluten particles at bay, but wooden utensils and cutting boards should be assigned to gluten-containing or g-free foods only. If you feel more comfortable keeping all dishes, utensils, and pots and pans for g-free foods separate, I would suggest a color-coding system. For example, a red cutting board, a red silicone spatula, a bread knife with red tape on the handle, and a red enameled skillet could all be used for gluten-free cooking and would be very easy to identify without confusion. For equipment that cannot be washed, such as the toaster, it's important to have separate toasters for gluten-free and regular breads. Alternatively, you can use one toaster oven but designate a toaster oven tray for gluten-free items only.

TIPS FOR COOKING SUCCESS

Now that we've got everything in place, it's time to get to the really good stuff—there are 100 really yummy and naturally gluten-free recipes waiting for you in the second half of this book, and I can't wait for you to cook them.

I want you to enjoy your time in the kitchen as much as I do, and I think that it's all in the approach. Here's my philosophy:

It's Just Food

We live in an age of food snobbery. You don't need to forage for your own mushrooms, own a six-burner Viking range, or know the difference between osetra and beluga caviar to cook amazing meals for your friends and family. Your impossibly small studio kitchen can still churn out impossibly delicious meals. I know plenty of people who don't cook because they find it intimidating or scary, but I've been cooking my whole life and I still make mistakes. It will happen, but it's the best way to learn. You'll get better with practice. Be sure to check out on the "How to Read a Recipe" section on page 60 if you're feeling nervous, and just take it step by step.

Eat What You Like

Have you ever heard anyone make definitive statements like, "Red wine goes with meat, white wine goes with fish"? In very general terms that may be so, but the way I see it, if you hate red wine, you aren't going to enjoy it with your steak regardless, right? When you cook at home, eat and cook what you like. If you don't like cilantro, you can still make the Sweet Mango Guacamole on page 108, just leave the cilantro out! Or if you hate pecans, just substitute almonds in the granola on page 78. Everyone's taste is different. Add that to the slew of common dietary restrictions out there, including gluten sensitivities, and you have plenty of reasons to justify changing a recipe, making substitutions, or omitting nonessential ingredients as you see fit. You are the boss in your kitchen!

Use the Best Ingredients

Using the best-quality ingredients will result in the best final product. If you have the budget for—and access to—local, organic ingredients, make them your first choice. They are the healthiest, tastiest choices and are better for the environment.

Stay Organized

Keeping an organized kitchen is imperative to making mealtimes easy. A few helpful suggestions:

- If you keep duplicates of items like cereal or milk on hand, organize by expiration date, keeping items that expire first in front of items that expire later so that they get used up sooner.
- Space savers like spice racks, lazy Susans, and plastic bag dispensers cost only a few dollars but can make a world of difference in keeping items easily accessible and organized.
- Keep items you use most often within easy reach. Your favorite sauté pan, a strainer, a whisk, a silicone spatula, and measuring cups and spoons are items you'll want at your fingertips every day.

Clean as You Go

Words to live by! Keeping a crumb-free kitchen is a must to avoid gluten contamination, and the last thing you want to worry about after preparing a beautiful meal is the pile of dishes in the sink. If you are waiting for water to boil, wipe down all the counters. Resting your meat before slicing it? Take the trash out, or do a few dishes. Thirty seconds here or there will make all the difference and keep you composed and feeling in control.

Make It Fun

It can and should be fun to cook at home. Don't take yourself so seriously, laugh off those mistakes, and have a blast. I keep an iPod dock in my kitchen so I have great music on hand at all times, too. If you will be spending the afternoon cooking for a dinner party, invite one or two friends to join you a bit early and help with the prep. Open a bottle of wine, crank up the music, and start the party early!

HOW TO READ A RECIPE

If you are just learning to cook, it's helpful to understand exactly how to navigate a recipe. Consider it your GPS to the perfect dish.

The first thing you should always do is read a recipe from start to finish. Make sure you have all of the ingredients you need, all of the proper equipment, and plenty of time to make the recipe.

Next, you will want to prep the ingredients. The ingredient list will show all of the ingredients needed to prepare the dish and, in most cookbooks and professional sources, they will be listed in the order that you will use them. You'll also find out how much of each ingredient you need and how to prep it, if any preliminary readying is required. When measuring your ingredients, pay special attention to the way the words are ordered. For example, 1 cup (110 g) chopped almonds means that you would chop your almonds first, then measure out 1 cup (110 g), whereas 1 cup (145 g) almonds, chopped means that you would measure out 1 cup (145 g) whole almonds first, and then chop them. This may seem like a trivial difference, but it can make a big change in the outcome of your final recipe. Just remember that the word that comes first signifies what you do first.

Once you have everything in place you can get started! Follow each step carefully and remember that cooking times are approximate, so look for other indicators of doneness, such as "bake until golden brown" or "cook until the onions have turned translucent" to guide you.

Recipe Jargon

If you're new to cooking, reading a recipe might seem foreign to you, because cooking has its own language. If you encounter any terms you aren't familiar with, refer to the list below, which includes definitions of some common cooking terms you may see in a recipe.

Bake: To cook in the oven with a dry, moderate heat and no direct exposure to a flame.

Baste: To brush a sauce, fats, or juices over meat during roasting. This will keep meat from drying out and add flavor.

Beat: To blend an ingredient or ingredients by vigorously whipping with a whisk, a fork, a spoon, or an electric mixer.

Blanch: To briefly immerse a food (usually produce) in boiling water. This technique is often used to bring out the green color of a vegetable.

Blend: To mix ingredients together to obtain a homogenous mixture.

Boil: To cook food in water or stock that is bubbling.

Braise: A cooking technique that involves slow, moist cooking in liquid.

This technique is often used to tenderize tough cuts of meat.

Broil: To cook food directly under a flame. This is typically listed as a setting on your oven. The broiler may be in the oven itself, or a drawer below the oven.

Deglaze: To add a small amount of liquid, such as wine or stock to a pan in which foods (usually meats) have been cooked. This liquid loosens the caramelized bits of food stuck to the bottom of the pan and helps incorporate them into a flavorful sauce.

Dice: To cut into small cubes.

Dredge: To coat a food evenly with a flour or cornstarch.

Fold: To gently combine a mixture by passing a spatula down through the center of the mixture, across the bottom, and up over the top, repeating as necessary to combine the ingredients, but keeping as much air in the mixture as possible.

Grate: To shred a food into fine pieces by running it along a microplane or grater.

Grease: To coat a pan or skillet with a thin layer of butter or oil to prevent ingredients from sticking.

Julienne: To cut into thin strips.

Marinate: To coat or immerse foods in a flavorful liquid. This adds flavor and can tenderize foods before cooking. The flavorful liquid is referred to as the marinade.

Mince: To cut into very tiny pieces.

Poach: A moist cooking technique where food is cooked slowly in a simmering liquid.

Purée: To mash or blend food until smooth and creamy.

Reduce: To cook a liquid down so that some of the moisture evaporates. This will reduce the liquid's volume, concentrate the flavors, and thicken the liquid.

Roast: A dry cooking method where food is cooked uncovered in the oven, usually at a higher heat than baking.

Sauté: To cook food quickly in a small amount of fat. This is done in a shallow pan on the stovetop over direct heat.

Score: To make shallow cuts across the surface of a food, sometimes in a crisscross pattern. This technique can be used to promote even cooking, crisp the fat or skin of a meat, tenderize meat, or allow for better absorption of a marinade.

Sear: To cook meat quickly over very high heat. This browns the outside and seals in juices.

Set: Allowing a food to solidify, usually by cooking or chilling.

Sift: Passing ingredients through a fine mesh to remove coarse particles. This process can also be used to blend different flours or starches. It introduces air into the ingredients.

Simmer: Cooking a liquid at a very low temperature so that only small bubbles gently break the surface.

Skim: Using a ladle to remove fat on the surface of stocks, soups, sauces, or other liquids.

Steam: To cook food suspended above boiling water (usually in a steamer basket) in a covered pot. The food does not come into direct contact with the liquid, which helps retain the flavor, shape, and nutrients of the food.

Water bath: To cook food by placing it into a vessel that is then set into a pan of simmering water. The pan is then placed in the oven, which allows the food to cook slowly and gently. Often used for custards or other dishes that need slow, even heat for cooking.

Whip: To incorporate air into ingredients, such as egg whites or cream, by whisking briskly until light and fluffy.

Whisk: To mix by beating vigorously. Usually done using a utensil of the same name.

Zest: The thin, outermost layer of the rind of citrus fruits, which contains oils with highly concentrated flavor. Use a microplane to remove the zest from citrus and finely grate it simultaneously.

Chapter

3

the
GLUTEN-FREE
FOOD DIRECTORY

There are hundreds and thousands of foods that do not contain gluten and are safe for you to eat, which I'll cover as thoroughly as possible in this chapter. As always, if you are having any doubts about a product or a food, always check with the manufacturer before using.

FOODS TO AVOID

Here's a list of what's strictly off-limits.

Baked goods
Barley
Biscuits
Bread
Brownies
Bulgur (made from wheat)
Cakes
Cookies
Cornbread
Crackers
Croutons
Cupcakes
Doughnuts
Durum (made from wheat)
Farro (species of wheat)
Kamut (species of wheat)
Matzo
Muffins
Pancakes
Pasta
Pastries
Pie crusts
Pizza
Pretzels
Rye
Seitan (meat alternative made with wheat gluten)
Semolina (made from wheat)
Spelt (species of wheat)
Stuffing
Triticale (hybrid of wheat and rye)
Waffles
Wheat

Hidden Offenders

Below is a list of ingredients that can contain gluten that might surprise you. I cannot stress enough the importance of reading labels!

Beer
Bouillon cubes
Bread crumbs (or anything battered or breaded and fried—or just fried in oil that also fries breaded items!)
Cereal (even corn or rice cereals can contain barley malt)
Chewing gum
Chips (even corn or potato chips can have gluten in the seasoning; multigrain varieties can contain wheat)
Cold cuts
Communion wafers
Energy bars
Frosting (some canned varieties)
Gravies
Ice cream (particularly with cookie or cake pieces)
Imitation seafood
Licorice
Malt vinegar
Malted milk/milkshakes
Marinades
Meat substitutes
Pie fillings
Salami
Sausages
Seasoned rice mixes (particularly the ones containing vermicelli pasta)
Self-basting turkey or chicken
Soup and soup bases (some popular brands contain hydrolyzed wheat protein)
Soy sauce
Teriyaki sauce
Worcestershire sauce (some brands contain soy sauce)

OAT NOTE

Oats are gluten-free, but regular oats are often processed in a facility that processes gluten-containing grains and can therefore become contaminated. Look for oats that are labeled gluten-free —they are grown far from gluten-containing grains and are harvested, processed, stored, and transported via gluten-free equipment and facilities. Oats that are labeled gluten-free are considered safe for those on a gluten free diet, although some with celiac still seem not to tolerate oats well.

Food Additives

Today, most food additives have no traceable amounts of gluten and are considered safe. Things like modified food starch and hydrolyzed vegetable protein, once thought to be unsafe, are now accepted as g-free. Of course, if you have any doubt, contact the manufacturer directly.

It's also important to note, however, that some additives, even though they are gluten-free, can still cause gastrointestinal upset for some individuals, especially if your body is still healing. Gluten isn't the only thing that can give you a stomachache, after all! Sorbitol, for example, a sugar substitute often used in chewing gum, mints, and cough syrup, tends to have a laxative effect and although it does not contain gluten, it may cause intestinal discomfort, especially for celiac sufferers with intestinal damage. Inulin, a derivative of chicory used to add fiber to foods, can also upset your stomach. Xanthan gum, often used in gluten-free baked goods, is another example (note that none of the recipes in this book contains this ingredient).

Health and Beauty Products

You may be wondering whether you should be concerned about ingredients in your health and beauty products. Research suggests that to have an immune reaction to gluten, you need to ingest the item, not just have skin contact with it. Shampoo, lotions, cosmetics, and other body products shouldn't present a problem, but wash your hands thoroughly after use to avoid ingesting them accidentally if you touch your mouth or face. Anything that comes close to your mouth, such as lipstick and lip balm, mouthwash, and toothpaste should be checked carefully for gluten ingredients. It's also a good idea to avoid putting products with gluten ingredients anywhere near open cuts or rashes, particularly dermatitis herpetiformis (a skin condition associated with celiac disease).

It can be tough to decipher health and beauty product ingredient labels, but look out for anything containing the words wheat, barley, or rye, as well as oat ingredients, which may be contaminated. Also look out for these hidden offenders:
- Amino-peptide complex (barley-derived)
- Avena sativa (oat-derived)
- Hordeum vulgare (barley-derived)
- Triticum vulgare (wheat-derived)
- Vitamin E and tocopherol (may be derived from wheat, so be sure to check!)

Gluten in Medications

Although few medications contain gluten, when it comes to your over-the-counter and prescription medications, it can be extremely difficult to determine whether they are, in fact, gluten-free. The problem is that there are no requirements or standards for gluten-free labeling of these products, and some fillers and inactive ingredients (usually made from starch) can be derived from gluten-containing ingredients. If the medication isn't specifically labeled gluten-free (I've only seen some vitamins and supplements labeled this way) it can be extremely hard to tell whether it is.

Look out for additives such as dextrates, dextrins, dextri-maltose, maltodextrin, malt, pregelatinized starch, and sodium starch glycolate, because these may contain gluten. If you have questions or concerns about your medications, ask your pharmacist or contact the pharmaceutical company directly. Ask questions not only about the ingredients, but also about the possibility of cross-contamination during the manufacturing process. If you still have doubts about a specific drug, contact your doctor to see whether there is a comparable alternative available.

Finally, be sure to ask your pharmacist and all of your doctors to note in your file that you cannot have medications with gluten.

NOT ALL GENERIC "EQUIVALENTS" ARE JUST THAT

It's important to note that brand-name drugs and their generic counterparts may not contain the same fillers, just the same active ingredients, so if a brand-name drug is gluten-free, it does not guarantee that its generic equivalent is, and vice versa. Pharmaceutical companies may also change the formulation of their medications from time to time, so it is important to periodically check whether they've altered the formulation of your medication and changed its gluten-containing status.

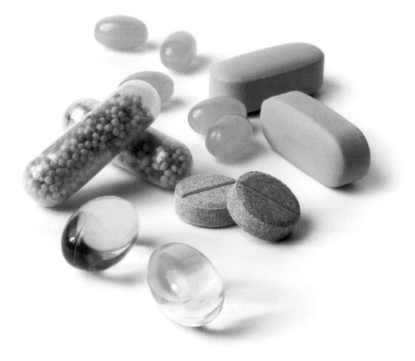

DIRECTORY OF NATURALLY GLUTEN-FREE FOODS

Now let's move on to the fun part—what you CAN eat! I've divided these lists into different food categories, to make navigation as seamless as possible. Use these lists to guide your shopping trips, or as a quick reference guide if you're unsure about something, or even as a quick pick-me-up when you're feeling like there's "nothing okay to eat." I guarantee it will pep you up!

Grains and Starches

The grains below are naturally gluten-free. Just make sure that they aren't processed in a facility that processes gluten ingredients.

Amaranth

Buckwheat

Corn

Millet

Montina (Indian ricegrass)

Oats labeled "gluten-free"

Quinoa

Rice

Sorghum

Teff

Wild rice

Flours

Make sure your flours are processed in a plant that does not process gluten ingredients in order to avoid cross-contamination. The label will likely say whether the flour was or was not.

Almond flour/meal

Amaranth flour

Arrowroot flour/starch/powder

Buckwheat flour

Cashew flour

Chestnut flour

Chickpea/garbanzo/besan flour

Coconut flour

Corn flour

Cornmeal flour

Cornstarch

Flaxseed meal

Gari (fermented cassava) flour

Guar gum

Hazelnut flour

Hemp seed flour/powder

Jerusalem artichoke flour

Kudzu starch

Millet flour

Pea (green) flour/starch

Pistachio flour

Plantain flour

Potato flour/starch

Pumpkin seed flour

Quinoa flour

Rice flour: white, brown, glutinous, or sweet

Sorghum flour

Soy (soya) flour

Tapioca flour

Taro root powder

Teff flour

Xanthan gum

Yam flour

Baking Ingredients

These common baking ingredients are naturally gluten-free. Check labels carefully to ensure these products have not been processed in a facility that processes gluten.

Agar agar

Baking powder (read labels carefully; some brands may contain wheat starch)

Baking soda

Cocoa

Egg replacer

Flax

Gelatin

Guar gum

Salt

Sugar

Vanilla

Vegetable shortening

Xanthan gum

Legumes

All legumes are naturally gluten-free, and canned varieties are typically safe.

Bean sprouts

Black beans

Black-eyed peas

Borlotti beans

Broad beans

Calico beans
Cannellini beans
Chickpeas
Edamame (soybeans)
Fava beans
Green beans
Italian beans
Kidney beans
Lentils
Lima beans
Mung beans
Navy beans
Peas
Pinto beans
Red beans

Nuts and Nut Butters

All nuts in their pure form are gluten-free; just watch out for those that contain added seasonings or other ingredients that may contain gluten (for example, pralines or candied nuts can sometimes contain wheat as an ingredient).

Almonds
Brazil nuts
Cashews
Hazelnuts
Macadamia nuts
Peanuts
Pecans
Pistachios

Proteins

This list isn't all inclusive, but generally, all plain animal proteins are gluten-free. You'll want to be wary of meats that come pre-marinated or have stock or some sort of moisture added (such as self-basting turkeys) because there can be gluten in these additives. Read labels on these items carefully. Also, avoid vegetarian proteins, like seitan and vegan meat substitutes, which are often made of wheat gluten.

■ CRUSTACEANS AND MOLLUSKS
Clams
Lobster
Mussels
Oysters
Shrimp
Snails

■ FISH
Anchovies
Angler
Bass
Bonefish
Carp
Catfish
Cod
Eel
Flounder
Herring
Perch
Roughy
Salmon
Sardines
Smelt
Snapper
Sole
Swordfish
Tilapia
Trout
Tuna

■ MEAT
Beef
Bison
Goat

Pork
Rabbit
Veal
Venison

■ POULTRY
Chicken
Duck
Goose
Ostrich
Pheasant
Quail
Turkey

■ VEGETARIAN PROTEINS
Tofu
Tempeh (be sure to check the label for wheat ingredients)

Produce

There are, of course, thousands of fruits and vegetables in the world— and the good news is that not one of them contains gluten! Here are just a few great varieties. Canned and frozen options are usually safe as well, but read the label to be sure.

■ FRUITS
Apples
Apricots
Avocados
Bananas
Blackberries
Blueberries
Currants
Cherries
Clementines
Dates (sometimes date pieces are rolled in oat flour, and those are not gluten-free unless labeled)
Eggplant

Elderberries
Grapes
Grapefruit
Guava
Huckleberries
Jicama
Kiwi
Kumquats
Lemons
Limes
Mandarins
Mangoes
Melons
Nectarines
Oranges
Peaches
Pears
Plums/prunes
Pineapple
Pomegranate
Raisins (dried grapes)
Raspberries
Red currants
Star fruit
Strawberries
Tangerines

■ VEGETABLES
Alfalfa sprouts
Artichoke
Arugula
Asparagus
Bok choy
Broccoli
Brussels sprouts
Cabbage
Carrots
Cauliflower
Celery
Chard
Cilantro
Collard greens
Corn

Cucumber
Endive
Fennel
Kale
Lemon grass
Lettuce
Mushrooms
Mustard greens
Nettles
Okra
Onion
Parsley
Peppers
Potatoes
Radicchio
Radish
Spinach
Squash
Sweet potatoes
Tomato
Water chestnut
Watercress
Yam

Dairy

All pure dairy products are gluten-free.

Butter, nondairy butters, and margarine
Buttermilk
Cream
Crème fraîche
Eggs
Evaporated milk
Ghee
Half-and-half
Kefir
Milk
Sour cream
Sweetened condensed milk
Whipped cream

Cheese

As a general rule, all cheeses are gluten-free. The exceptions are some exotic cheeses that are "washed" in beer or even rolled in bread crumbs, such as the French Sablé de Wissant, but if you are buying these fancy cheeses, you're probably at a cheese shop where there is someone who can answer any questions you have about how they are made.

Some blue cheeses may use bread starters for the mold. Generally, though, it's become accepted that even blue cheeses made with bread starters contain such trace amounts of gluten that they are undetectable when tested and won't make you sick.

American
Asiago
Blue cheese
Brie
Buffalo
Camembert
Cheddar
Colby
Cottage cheese
Cream cheese
Feta
Goat cheese
Gouda
Havarti
Jarlsberg
Mascarpone
Monterrey Jack
Mozzarella
Munster
Parmesan
Pecorino Romano

Provolone
Queso fresco
Ricotta
Swiss

Condiments

Barbecue sauce (some may contain soy sauce; read the label carefully)
Distilled vinegar
Guacamole
Horseradish
Hot sauce
Jam/jelly
Ketchup
Lemon juice
Lime juice
Mayonnaise
Mustard
Pesto
Pico de gallo
Salsa
Steak sauce (some, read the label for soy sauce or other wheat ingredients)
Tartar sauce

Dressings

Dressings can be tricky because they sometimes contain wheat ingredients or soy sauce, so always read the label!

French dressing
Greek dressing
Honey mustard
Italian dressing
Mayonnaise
Oil and vinegar
Ranch dressing
Russian dressing
Thousand Island dressing
Vinaigrettes

Spices

All spices are gluten-free, but read the label carefully to make sure they don't include noncaking agents with wheat ingredients.

Basil
Bay leaves
Caraway seed
Cardamom
Celery flakes
Celery seed
Chili powder
Chives
Cilantro
Cinnamon
Cloves
Coriander
Cumin
Curry powder
Dill seed
Fennel
Garlic, minced
Garlic pepper
Garlic powder
Garlic salt
Ginger
Hickory smoked salt
Italian seasoning
Jamaican jerk seasoning
Lemon and herb
Lemon pepper
Mace
Marjoram
Meat tenderizer
Mint leaves
Monosodium glutamate (MSG)
Mustard
Nutmeg
Onion, minced
Onion powder
Onion salt
Orange peel
Oregano
Paprika
Parsley
Pepper
Pepper, cayenne
Pepper, crushed red
Pickling spice
Poppy seed
Poultry seasoning
Pumpkin pie spice
Rosemary
Sage
Sesame seed
Tarragon
Thyme
Turmeric

SAFE SOY SAUCE

Soy sauce is made from fermented soybeans, but it usually also contains wheat! Japanese soy sauce, called tamari, is usually made exclusively from soybeans, without any wheat ingredients.

Always look for soy sauce or tamari that is specifically labeled gluten-free to ensure it is safe!

Drinks and Cocktails

Gluten is removed during the distillation process of alcohol, so any distilled alcoholic beverage (i.e., "hard liquor") made with wheat, barley, or rye is safe. Beer is not a distilled beverage and is therefore not safe because it contains barley hops or wheat ingredients (though there are a few gluten-free varieties popping up). Also watch out for malt beverages like wine coolers, which may be made with barley. If you're ordering a fancy cocktail at a lounge or restaurant, make sure it isn't made with any garnishes that contain gluten. I've seen graham cracker rims on drinks or candies placed inside of drinks that may be unsafe.

Bloody Marys often have Worcestershire sauce as an ingredient, and some Worcestershire sauce contains gluten. Ask the bartender to check for you!

■ ALCOHOLIC BEVERAGES

Absinthe
Amaretto
Bourbon
Brandy
Champagne
Cognac
Gin
Grappa
Hard cider (generally safe, but avoid those with malt ingredients)
Kirsch
Liqueurs
Madeira
Mezcal
Ouzo
Port
Rum
Sake
Scotch
Sherry
Tequila
Vermouth
Vodka
Whiskey
Wine

■ COCKTAIL GARNISHES

Cherry
Coconut
Cucumber
Ginger
Lemon
Lime
Olive
Pineapple
Salt
Sugar

■ COCKTAIL MIXERS

Angostura bitters
Blue curaçao
Coconut cream
Cola
Fruit juice
Grenadine
Lemon juice
Lime juice
Margarita mix
Simple syrup
Soda water
Sour mix
Triple sec
Vegetable juice

■ NONALCOHOLIC BEVERAGES

Chocolate milk
Coffee
Cola
Diet cola
Fruit juice
Fruit smoothies
Hot chocolate
Iced coffee
Iced tea
Lemonade
Milk
Soda water
Tea
Vegetable juice

Candies and Packaged Snacks

....

Below is a list of some easy-to-find, gluten-free packaged snacks and candies. This list is not all-inclusive but is meant to give you an idea of the variety of snacks you can still have. If you don't see your favorite snack or candy on the list, read the label or contact the manufacturer with your questions. Keep in mind that manufacturers often change recipe formulations and processing methods, so even if you think something is gluten-free, always check carefully before consuming any packaged foods because its gluten-containing status can change at any time. Even the products on this list may change if a manufacturer revises its formula or recipe.

■ CANDY

3 Musketeers
Andes mints
Baby Ruth
Betty Crocker, Fruit Roll-Ups, Fruit Shapes
Bit-O-Honey
Butterfinger, original
Cella's chocolate-covered cherries
Charleston Chew
Charms Candy Carnival
Charms Caramel Apple Pops, Blow Pops, Flat Pops, Mini Pops
Clark Bar
Cliff Kid Organic Twisted Fruit
Dots
Goobers

Haribo Gold Bears, Clown Fish, minis, tubs
Haviland Thin Mints
Jelly Belly jellybeans
Junior Mints
Necco Wafers
Nestlé milk chocolate
Oh Henry!
Pez, all varieties
Raisinets
Razzles
Skittles, Sour, Wild Berry, Crazy Cores
Sno-Caps
Spangler Candy Canes, Chewy Canes
Spangler Circus Peanuts
Spangler Dum Dums, Dum Dums Chewy Pops
Spangler Saf-T-Pops
Sugar Babies
Sugar Daddy
Sweethearts Conversation Hearts
Tootsie Pops
Tootsie Rolls
Trident gum
Welch's Fruit Snacks
Wonka Fun Dip
Wonka Laffy Taffy
Wonka Pixy Stix
Wrigley's gum, all varieties

■ SNACKS

Blue Diamond Nut Thins, all varieties
Cheetos Puffs, Honey BBQ, Simply Natural
Chex, Cinnamon, Chocolate, Corn, Rice, Honey Nut
Edy's fruit bars and sherbet
Frito's corn chips, Original, Lightly Salted
Jell-O gelatin and Pudding Snacks
Jolly Time popcorn, all varieties
Kind Bars, all varieties
Kozy Shack, puddings, flans, gels
Larabars, all varieties
Lay's potato chips, Classic, Lightly Salted, Simply Natural, Baked Original, Wavy Original
Lay's Stax chips, all varieties
Pirate Brands Pirate's Booty, all varieties
Pirate Brands Potato Flyers, all varieties
Pirate Brands Smart Puffs
Ruffles potato chips, Original, Reduced Fat, Smokehouse Style BBQ, Simply Natural Reduced Fat Sea Salted, Baked Original
Sabra hummus, all varieties
Santitas tortilla chips, all varieties
Stonyfield yogurt, all varieties except Yo Toddler
Tostitos, Restaurant Style, Bite Size, Crispy Rounds, Scoops, Simply Natural

Eating Out

Below is a general guideline to help you identify menu items that are typically gluten-free at different types of restaurants. Always check with your server about possible gluten ingredients and cross-contamination.

■ SAFE OPTIONS: CHINESE

Your choices when eating out at a Chinese restaurant are often very limited because most soy sauces contain gluten, but you can order something made without it and bring your own g-free soy sauce along! You can even find travel-friendly disposable packets (similar to ketchup packets) online. Following are some other options that are generally safe:

Fried rice (without soy sauce)
Meat dishes (white or clear sauces only)
Rice noodles
Steamed rice
Steamed vegetables

■ SAFE OPTIONS: DINERS

Baked, broiled, or steamed fish
Burgers (no bun)
Chicken, roasted or grilled
Cottage cheese and fruit
Eggs and omelets
Hash browns
Salads (no croutons)
Vegetables

■ SAFE OPTIONS: ITALIAN

Eating out at an Italian restaurant can be tricky. Watch for pitfalls like breaded meats, eggplant, and fish, and of course, pastas and pizza.

Grilled fish
Grilled vegetables
Marinara sauce
Meats with no breading
Mozzarella cheese and tomato salad (caprese)
Polenta
Risotto
Salads (no croutons)
Steamed mussels or clams

■ SAFE OPTIONS: JAPANESE

When eating sushi, watch out for imitation crab, which often contains wheat as a binder. Eel sauce also generally contains gluten, and spicy rolls often have tempura flakes mixed in, so be sure to specify no tempura flakes in your rolls. And don't forget to bring your own g-free soy sauce bottle or packets for dipping.

Edamame
Sashimi
Seaweed salad
Steamed rice
Sushi (some)

■ SAFE OPTIONS: MEXICAN

Happily, most Mexican restaurant menu items are safe. Just beware of anything that is made with flour tortillas—burritos and taco salad bowls included.

Corn tortillas (not flour)
Enchiladas
Guacamole
Huevos rancheros
Meats (without breading)
Refried beans
Salads
Salsa
Tacos
Tortilla chips
Vegetable dishes

CARE PACKAGE PROGRAM

The University of Chicago Celiac Disease Center offers gluten-free care packages to the newly diagnosed. The basket is full of helpful resources and food samples to introduce people with celiac disease to a gluten-free diet. The university also has an information hotline to answer any questions you may have. It gives you access to experts who can answer your questions about symptoms, testing, diagnosis, treatment, and follow-up care. Call 773-702-7593 to request a care package or access the information hotline.

ADDITIONAL RESOURCES

If you are looking for additional support and resources, the Internet is your oyster! Here are just a few of the websites I find helpful.

- **Celiac Disease Foundation**, www.celiac.org
- **Celiac Sprue Association**, www.csaceliacs.info: includes resources to help you find a celiac support group near you.
- **EZ Gluten**, www.ezgluten.com: offers test strips that can detect gluten at levels of 10 parts per million in foods you may be unsure are safe; they are a bit pricy—$25 for a two-pack—but can offer real peace of mind if you are unsure about a dish.
- **GlutenFree.com**, www.glutenfree.com: offers hundreds of gluten-free packaged foods you might not be able to find in a store near you.
- **Gluten-Free Mall**, www.celiac.com/glutenfreemall: another resource where you can find lots of gluten-free packaged products all in one place.
- **Gluten Free Registry**, www.glutenfreeregistry.com: an interactive website for finding gluten-free restaurants and businesses in your state; also available as a mobile app.
- **Gluten Intolerance Group**, www.gluten.net
- **Honeyville**, www.store.honeyvillegrain.com: offers gluten-free flours, including almond flour, which can be used in some of the baking recipes in this book.

Phone Apps for the Tech-Savvy G-Free

For those with smart phones, here are just a few great apps you may want to consider downloading for instant gluten-free assistance while you're out and about.

- **ScanAvert:** This app for iPhones lets you take a picture of the bar code on an item, and it will tell you whether the item is gluten-free. It will even offer an alternative recommendation if the item you scan is incompatible with a gluten-free diet.
- **Find Me Gluten Free:** This Android app uses your GPS to locate gluten-free-friendly coffee shops, groceries, bars, and restaurants near you. You can check out menus, get the phone number, and even find directions to each business.
- **Cook It Allergy Free:** Available for iPhones and iPads, this cookbook app features hundreds of recipes that home cooks can use to accommodate all kinds of dietary restrictions (great if you have allergies or sensitivities to more than just gluten!). You can save recipes offline for use any time and even make a grocery list organized by aisle.
- **Gluten Free Restaurant Cards from CeliacTravel.com:** Doing some traveling? This app has restaurant cards similar to the one in this book (page 47) in languages like Spanish, Italian, Korean, Latvian, Norwegian, and more. Pull up the card you need, and show it to your server directly from your iPhone or iPad.

PART 2

NATURALLY GLUTEN-FREE RECIPES

Chapter

4

DELICIOUS *ways to* START THE DAY

Fruit Salad with Minted Simple Syrup

*The mint in this beautifully colored fruit salad really brings to life the flavors of the fruit.
It's incredibly refreshing but still subtle. Top with whipped cream, if desired.*

FOR MINTED SIMPLE SYRUP:

3   TABLESPOONS (18 G) CHOPPED
    FRESH MINT, PLUS MORE FOR
    GARNISH (OPTIONAL)

¼   CUP (50 G) SUGAR

¼   CUP (60 ML) WATER

FOR SALAD:

1   CUP (145 G) BLUEBERRIES

1   CUP (170 G) SLICED STRAWBERRIES

1   CUP (175 G) PEELED, DICED MANGO

2   KIWIS, PEELED AND SLICED

1   CUP (125 G) RASPBERRIES

1   GRAPEFRUIT, PEELED AND SEGMENTED

To make the syrup: In a small saucepan over medium heat, combine the mint, sugar, and water. Bring to a boil, stirring, until the sugar has dissolved and the liquid has reduced slightly, about 3 minutes. Remove from the heat and allow to steep for 10 minutes. Strain out the mint and discard. Let cool to room temperature.

In a large bowl, combine the salad ingredients. Add the minted simple syrup and toss until combined. Garnish with additional mint if desired.

YIELD: 6 SERVINGS

CHEF'S TIP *Use whatever fruit is in season and looks best to you at the market. Choose a variety of colors and textures for the best presentation!*

All-Natural Homemade Yogurt

Making homemade products is a great way to control the quality of your food. There are no added preservatives, thickeners, sugars, or chemicals in this yogurt. Homemade yogurt is simple and economical, and it tastes great. Use this yogurt (pictured in jar on page 79) to make the Vanilla, Almond, and Date Smoothies on page 78 or Grilled Lamb Kebabs with Creamy Tzatziki Sauce on page 150.

4   CUPS (940 ML) MILK

¼   CUP (60 G) PLAIN YOGURT

Preheat the oven to its lowest setting (warm).

Heat the milk in a medium saucepan over medium-low heat. Use a candy thermometer to check the temperature until the milk reaches 190°F (88°C). Remove the milk from the heat. Allow to cool to 120°F (49°C), then whisk in the yogurt until combined. Heat a large stockpot filled halfway with water to 120°F (49°C).

Pour the mixture into one or more glass jars and place the lid on tight. Put the jar(s) into the stockpot with warm water (they should be immersed in water but not covered to the top in case your jars are not watertight). Cover the stockpot, wrap it in an old towel to insulate it, and place in the warm oven. Turn the oven off.

Let the yogurt mixture sit for 4 to 8 hours, or until it thickens (depending on the yogurt starter you use, it may take longer to thicken, so check on it periodically).

The yogurt will also thicken some more once it is completely cooled. Chill and store in the refrigerator for up to 3 weeks.

YIELD: 4 CUPS (940 ML)

✗ CHEF'S TIPS *Here's an alternative method if you have a slow cooker. After combining and heating the yogurt and milk in the saucepan, pour the mixture into the unplugged slow cooker, cover with the lid, wrap in a towel, and let sit for 4 to 8 hours. Then spoon into containers and chill. ■ For thicker Greek-style yogurt, line a fine-mesh strainer with 4 layers of cheesecloth, and set it over a bowl. Place the finished yogurt into the strainer, and let sit in the refrigerator for 2 hours to drain excess liquid from the yogurt. Discard the liquid and place the strained yogurt back into the jar until ready to use.*

✚ VARIATION *For fruit-on-the-bottom-style yogurt, place 1 to 2 tablespoons (20 to 40 g) of jam on the bottom of four 8-ounce (225-g) containers, then top with the milk mixture and leave it to culture for 4 to 8 hours.*

Vanilla, Almond, and Date Smoothie

Smoothies are fast, easy, and filling. This tart, creamy smoothie (pictured in foreground) has no added sugar but is perfectly sweet thanks to the dates.

¼ CUP (60 G) PLAIN YOGURT, STORE-BOUGHT OR HOMEMADE (PAGE 77),

1 TABLESPOON (16 G) ALMOND BUTTER

5 DATES, PITTED

1 CUP (235 ML) UNSWEETENED ALMOND MILK

¼ TEASPOON VANILLA EXTRACT

5 ICE CUBES

Place all the ingredients in a blender. Start by blending on low and gradually increase the speed. Blend until smooth. Pour into 2 glasses and serve.

YIELD: 2 SERVINGS

+ VARIATION *You can use unsweetened vanilla flavored almond milk instead of adding vanilla extract if you like.*

Flax and Pecan Granola

Homemade granola is so simple, I can't think of a single reason to buy it from the store. The key is to cook it at a low temperature to keep the maple syrup from burning. I like to use a combination of dark and golden raisins.

2 CUPS (220 G) CHOPPED PECANS

4 CUPS (320 G) GLUTEN-FREE ROLLED OATS

1 CUP (85 G) FLAKED COCONUT

1 CUP (140 G) PEPITAS (PUMPKIN SEEDS)

½ CUP (56 G) FLAXSEED MEAL

2 TABLESPOONS (30 G) BROWN SUGAR

⅛ TEASPOON SALT

½ CUP (120 ML) PURE MAPLE SYRUP

2 TEASPOONS VANILLA EXTRACT

¼ CUP (60 ML) CANOLA OIL

2 CUPS (290 G) RAISINS

Preheat the oven to 300°F (150°C, or gas mark 2). Grease 2 rimmed baking sheets and set aside.

In a large bowl, combine the pecans, oats, coconut, pepitas, flaxseed meal, brown sugar, salt, maple syrup, vanilla, and canola oil. Stir to coat all of the ingredients well with the maple syrup.

Pour onto the greased baking sheets and spread into an even layer. Bake for 40 minutes, stirring occasionally to prevent over-browning of the granola at the edges.

Remove the granola from the oven, stir in the raisins, and let cool. Store in an airtight container for up to 2 weeks.

YIELD: ABOUT 10 ½ CUPS (1280 G), OR 21 SERVINGS (½ CUP [61 G] EACH)

Eggs Florentine
(Poached Eggs over Wilted Spinach with Creamy Sauce)

*Hollandaise is an incredibly easy sauce to make despite its fussy French roots,
but let everyone you serve it to believe that you toiled over a hot stove for hours!*

FOR CREAMY SAUCE:

2   EGG YOLKS

½   CUP (112 G) UNSALTED BUTTER, MELTED

1   TABLESPOON (15 ML) LEMON JUICE
    PINCH OF CAYENNE
    SALT AND PEPPER TO TASTE

FOR EGGS AND SPINACH:

1   TEASPOON OLIVE OIL

8   CUPS (240 G) BABY SPINACH
    SALT AND PEPPER TO TASTE

1   TABLESPOON (15 ML) WHITE VINEGAR

4   EGGS

✖ **CHEF'S TIP** *To make the creamy
sauce in a blender, place the egg
yolks, lemon juice, cayenne, and
a pinch of salt and pepper to the
blender. Blend until smooth. With
the blender on high, gradually pour
in the melted butter. The sauce
should be thick and smooth.*

To make the sauce: Make a double boiler by filling a medium saucepan with 3 inches (7.5 cm) of water. Bring to a boil over high heat, then reduce the heat to low. In a small heat-proof mixing bowl that is large enough to sit on top of the saucepan without touching it, whisk the egg yolks lightly. Place over the saucepan with the simmering water. The bottom of the mixing bowl should be at least 2 inches (5 cm) from the water. Continue whisking over the heat until the yolks have thickened enough to coat the back of a spoon, about 2 or 3 minutes.

Very slowly, stream in the melted butter while continuously whisking to form a rich, smooth sauce. Add the lemon juice, cayenne, and salt and pepper to taste. Turn off the heat, cover loosely with plastic wrap, and leave the bowl over the hot water to stay warm while you prepare the other elements of the dish.

To make the eggs and spinach: In a large sauté pan, heat the oil over medium heat. Add the spinach and sauté until wilted, about 2 minutes. Season with salt and pepper to taste and set aside.

Fill a medium saucepan halfway with water. Add the white vinegar and bring to a simmer over medium heat. Crack an egg into a small bowl or ramekin, being careful not to break the yolk. Gently pour the egg into the simmering water. Immediately, with a wooden spoon, slowly stir the water around the egg gently a few times to create a circular wave to help keep the white of the egg from spreading. Cook the egg until the whites have set but the yolk is still soft, about 3 minutes. With a slotted spoon, remove the egg and let drain on a paper towel. Repeat the process with remaining 3 eggs.

To serve, divide the spinach among 4 plates. Place 1 egg onto each pile of spinach. Spoon the hollandaise sauce over each egg, about 2 tablespoons (30 g) per egg.

◼ **YIELD: 4 SERVINGS**

Baked Eggs with Tomato and Bell Pepper Marmalade

With a little TLC, you can simply and easily coax peppers, onions, and tomatoes into a luscious, sweet marmalade. Layered with salty Virginia ham and topped with tender baked eggs, this beautiful dish is one you will make again and again.

6   THIN SLICES VIRGINIA HAM

1   TABLESPOON (15 ML) OLIVE OIL

1   CUP (150 G) DICED RED BELL PEPPER

1   CUP (150 G) DICED GREEN BELL PEPPER

1   CUP (160 G) DICED WHITE ONION

    SALT AND PEPPER TO TASTE

1   CUP (180 G) DICED TOMATO

6   EGGS

> ✗ **CHEF'S TIP** *In a hurry? Although you won't get the sweet caramelized flavor and texture of the marmalade if you cook the vegetables quickly, they are still delish with just a quick sauté to soften them up before layering them with the other ingredients.*

Preheat the oven to 350°F (180°C, or gas mark 4). Place six 6-ounce (170-g) ramekins in a baking dish, such as a lasagna pan. Grease the ramekins, then place 1 slice of ham into each one. Set aside.

Heat a medium nonstick sauté pan over medium heat. Add the olive oil, red and green bell pepper, and onion to the pan. Season with salt and pepper, cover, and cook for 17 to 20 minutes, stirring occasionally, until the vegetables have softened and begin to caramelize and turn lightly brown and sweet. If the mixture gets too dry or starts to get too brown in some spots, add 1 tablespoon (15 ml) of water to the pan and keep cooking.

Add the diced tomato and cook an additional 5 to 7 minutes over medium heat, but this time leave the pan uncovered to reduce some of the liquid from the tomatoes. When the mixture is thick and begins to resemble a marmalade texture (think chunky jam), it is finished. Remove from the heat.

Divide the mixture evenly among the 6 ramekins. Crack 1 egg into each ramekin on top of the marmalade mixture. Sprinkle with a pinch of salt, then fill the baking dish with hot water. Bake for 20 to 25 minutes, or until the white of the egg is set and the yolk is still soft. Serve immediately.

◼ **YIELD: 6 SERVINGS**

Flank Steak with Chimichurri and Eggs

Chimichurri is a traditional Argentine sauce served with grilled meat. It is pungent and tangy and is delicious with flank steak. I serve this with the Fruit Salad with Minted Simple Syrup on page 76 and the Potato and Parsnip Home Fries on page 90 for a stunning brunch that is sure to impress!

FOR CHIMICHURRI SAUCE:

1	LARGE CLOVE GARLIC
½	CUP (30 G) PACKED FRESH PARSLEY
½	CUP (120 ML) EXTRA-VIRGIN OLIVE OIL
1	TEASPOON RED WINE VINEGAR
¼	TEASPOON RED PEPPER FLAKES
	SALT AND PEPPER TO TASTE

FOR STEAK AND EGGS:

1½	POUNDS (680 G) FLANK STEAK
2	TEASPOONS BUTTER, DIVIDED
8	EGGS, DIVIDED

CHEF'S TIP *Slice the steak across the grain for tenderness. The meat has long fibers that you can see. "Across the grain" means that you slice the meat across the fibers, which will make the steak more tender and easier to chew.*

To make the sauce: In a food processor, pulse the whole garlic clove until chopped. Add the parsley, and pulse to chop. Add the olive oil, red wine vinegar, and red pepper flakes, and pulse 3 or 4 times until blended into a thick sauce. Transfer the chimichurri sauce to a bowl and season to taste with salt and pepper. (The sauce can be made a day in advance.) Set aside.

To make the steak and eggs: Preheat a grill or broiler on high. Season the steak generously on both sides with salt and pepper. Grill or broil for about 3 minutes per side for medium-rare, or until it reaches your desired doneness. Transfer the meat to a cutting board and cover with aluminum foil to keep warm.

In a large nonstick skillet, melt 1 teaspoon of the butter over medium heat. Crack 4 of the eggs into the pan, taking care not to break the yolks. Season with salt and pepper and cook for 3 to 4 minutes, or until they begin to set, then flip them over and cook for about 20 seconds more for over-easy eggs or longer to set the yolks if you prefer. Transfer the eggs, 2 per person, to separate plates, then repeat with the remaining 4 eggs and the remaining 1 teaspoon butter.

To serve, thinly slice the steak, then divide it among the plates. Spoon the chimichurri over the steak and serve immediately.

YIELD: 4 SERVINGS

Huevos Rancheros

This hearty morning breakfast made with tortillas, eggs, beans, and salsa is packed with flavor as well as protein and fiber, which will keep you fueled for hours.

1 TABLESPOON (15 ML) PLUS 2 TEASPOONS (10 ML) CANOLA OIL, DIVIDED

2 SOFT CORN TORTILLAS

⅔ CUP (170 G) REFRIED BEANS, STORE-BOUGHT OR HOMEMADE (PAGE 178), WARMED

4 EGGS

SALT AND PEPPER TO TASTE

¼ CUP (65 G) SALSA OF YOUR CHOICE, DIVIDED

¼ CUP (60 G) SOUR CREAM OR MEXICAN CREMA, DIVIDED

2 SCALLIONS, THINLY SLICED

In a large nonstick or cast-iron skillet, heat 1 tablespoon (15 ml) of the canola oil over medium-high heat. Fry each corn tortilla for about 1 minute on each side, or until crispy. Place each tortilla onto a plate. Top each with half of the refried beans. Set aside and keep warm.

In the same pan, heat the remaining 2 teaspoons (10 ml) oil over medium heat. Crack the eggs into the pan, taking care not to break the yolks. Season with salt and pepper and cook until the eggs are set enough to be able to flip, about 2 minutes. Cook for 30 seconds on the other side. Use a spatula to transfer 2 eggs on top of the beans on each plate.

Top each plate of eggs with half of the salsa and half of the sour cream. Garnish with the scallions, and serve immediately.

◤ YIELD: 2 SERVINGS

CHEF'S TIP *If you don't have corn tortillas, try serving this over tortilla chips!*

Stovetop Oatmeal with Fresh Blueberry Maple Syrup

Oatmeal is the perfect breakfast to keep you full and satisfied all morning long.
A swirl of blueberry syrup adds the perfect sweetness.

FOR OATMEAL:

1½   **CUPS (120 G) GLUTEN-FREE OATS**

2   **CUPS (470 ML) WATER**

1   **CUP (235 ML) MILK OR ALMOND MILK**

2   **TABLESPOONS (30 G) LIGHT BROWN SUGAR**

PINCH OF SALT

FOR BLUEBERRY MAPLE SYRUP:

1   **CUP (145 G) FRESH OR FROZEN BLUEBERRIES**

¼   **CUP (60 ML) MAPLE SYRUP**

½   **TEASPOON GROUND CINNAMON**

To make the oatmeal: Combine the oats, water, milk, brown sugar, and salt in a heavy-bottomed pot. Bring to a boil over medium-high heat, then reduce the heat to medium-low and cook for about 10 minutes, or until most of the liquid has been absorbed and the oatmeal is thick.

To make the blueberry syrup: While the oatmeal cooks, combine the blueberries, maple syrup, and ground cinnamon in a small saucepan and bring to a boil over medium-high heat. Some of the blueberries will begin to burst and release their juices. Remove from the heat.

Spoon the oatmeal into 6 bowls, then top with the syrup. Serve immediately.

YIELD: 6 SERVINGS

> **CHEF'S TIP** *Use leftover blueberry maple syrup as a topping for ice cream. Heaven!*

Sweet Potato and Mushroom Hash

You can use any mushrooms that you like in this recipe (pictured at right). For every day, I use button or cremini mushrooms, but to make this dish more special, I'll use chanterelles, oyster, or trumpet mushrooms.

1	TABLESPOON (15 ML) OLIVE OIL
2	CUPS (140 G) SLICED MUSHROOMS
·	SALT AND PEPPER TO TASTE
2	LARGE (ABOUT 2 POUNDS, OR 908 G) SWEET POTATOES, PEELED AND DICED
1	CUP (160 G) DICED ONION
1	CUP (150 G) DICED GREEN BELL PEPPER
3	CLOVES GARLIC, MINCED
1	TEASPOON GARLIC POWDER

Preheat the oven to 375°F (190°C, or gas mark 5). Heat the oil in a large oven-safe nonstick skillet over medium-high heat. Add the mushrooms to the pan, season with salt and pepper, and cook for 5 to 6 minutes, or until they release their juices and become golden brown.

Stir in the sweet potato, onion, bell pepper, minced garlic, and garlic powder. Season with salt and pepper and transfer the pan to the oven.

Bake for 25 to 30 minutes, or until the sweet potatoes are browned on the outside and soft all the way through.

YIELD: 6 SERVINGS

Maple Turkey Breakfast Sausage

I bet you had no idea that making your own sausages (pictured at right, with hash) could be so easy! Try substituting ground chicken for the turkey and add about ¼ cup (60 g) finely diced sautéed apple to the mixture for chicken and apple sausage.

1	POUND (455 G) GROUND TURKEY (WHITE OR DARK MEAT, BOTH WORK WELL)
2	TABLESPOONS (30 ML) MAPLE SYRUP
2	TABLESPOONS (30 ML) OLIVE OIL, DIVIDED
½	TEASPOON GARLIC POWDER
¼	TEASPOON ONION POWDER
¼	TEASPOON DRIED SAGE
1½	TEASPOONS SALT
½	TEASPOON FRESHLY GROUND BLACK PEPPER

Combine the turkey, maple syrup, 1 tablespoon (15 ml) of the olive oil, garlic powder, onion powder, dried sage, salt, and pepper in a mixing bowl. Using wet hands, shape the turkey mixture into twelve 2-inch (5-cm) patties.

Preheat a sauté pan over medium heat. Add the remaining 1 tablespoon (15 ml) olive oil. Add the turkey sausage patties and sauté for about 4 minutes per side, until evenly browned and cooked through.

YIELD: 12 SAUSAGE PATTIES

Potato and Parsnip Home Fries

These baked home fries get an added boost of flavor and nutrition from the parsnips, which become caramelized and sweet when roasted. Use the free stovetop space for making eggs or other breakfast goodies.

1½ POUNDS (680 G) WAXY POTATOES, CUT INTO SMALL CUBES

½ POUND (225 G) PARSNIPS, PEELED AND CUT INTO SMALL CUBES

1 TABLESPOON (15 ML) OLIVE OIL

SALT AND PEPPER TO TASTE

1 RED OR GREEN BELL PEPPER, STEMMED, SEEDED, AND DICED

½ WHITE ONION, DICED

½ TEASPOON GARLIC POWDER

½ TEASPOON ONION POWDER

½ TEASPOON PAPRIKA

Preheat the oven to 400°F (200°C, or gas mark 6). On a nonstick baking sheet or one lined with parchment paper, toss together the potatoes, parsnips, olive oil, and a pinch of salt. Bake for 15 minutes.

Add the bell pepper, onion, garlic powder, onion powder, and paprika, and toss until well combined. Bake for another 20 minutes, or until golden and cooked through. Season with salt and pepper to taste and serve hot.

YIELD: 6 SERVINGS

Asparagus and Tomato Frittata

A frittata is simply a big open-faced omelet. It makes a great vehicle for using up all kinds of leftovers. Vegetables, meats, cheeses, herbs . . . the possibilities are endless, so add in what you like!

2 TABLESPOONS (30 ML) OLIVE OIL

½ WHITE ONION, THINLY SLICED

1 BUNCH ASPARAGUS, TOUGH ENDS REMOVED, DICED

8 EGGS

½ TEASPOON SALT

¼ TEASPOON FRESHLY GROUND BLACK PEPPER

2 TOMATOES, SLICED

Preheat the oven to 350°F (180°C, or gas mark 4).

In a 10-inch (25-cm) sauté pan or cast-iron skillet, heat the olive oil over medium heat. Add the onion and the asparagus and sauté until they just begin to get tender, about 3 minutes.

In a large mixing bowl, whisk the eggs, salt, and pepper. Add the beaten eggs to the pan, and continue to cook over medium heat until the bottom and sides begin to set, about another 3 to 4 minutes. Turning the heat too high will make your eggs rubbery.

Arrange the sliced tomatoes on top, then transfer to the oven and bake for about 15 minutes, or until the center is completely set and the edges are golden. Serve hot or at room temperature.

YIELD: 6 SERVINGS

Chapter

5

SWEET *and* SAVORY STARTERS *and* SNACKS

Sriracha and Honey–Glazed Chicken Wings

These sweet and sticky wings have a hint of heat and a huge punch of flavor.
They're great for game day, or even packed for a picnic.

6   CLOVES GARLIC, MINCED, DIVIDED

1   INCH (2.5-CM) PIECE GINGER, MINCED, DIVIDED

½   CUP (120 ML) FRESH SQUEEZED ORANGE JUICE

2   TABLESPOONS (30 ML) SESAME OIL, DIVIDED

1   TEASPOON SALT

3   POUNDS (1365 G) CHICKEN WINGS

1   TABLESPOON (14 G) BUTTER

1   TABLESPOON (6 G) ORANGE ZEST

½   CUP (170 G) HONEY

2   TABLESPOONS (28 G) SRIRACHA SAUCE

1   TABLESPOON (8 G) SESAME SEEDS

> ✗ **CHEF'S TIP** *If you prefer crispy wings to sticky wings, you can deep-fry them for about 5 minutes in hot oil, or until cooked through. Then just toss the hot wings with the honey mixture, sprinkle with the sesame seeds, and serve.*

In a small bowl, combine about half of the minced garlic and half of the ginger with the orange juice, 1 tablespoon (15 ml) of the sesame oil, and the salt. Pour the mixture over the chicken wings and marinate at room temperature for 1 hour, or up to overnight in the fridge.

To make the sauce for the wings, melt the butter in a small saucepan over medium heat. Add the remaining half of the ginger and garlic and cook for 2 to 3 minutes to soften the garlic. Add the orange zest, honey, and sriracha, and cook another 1 to 2 minutes to combine the flavors.

After the wings are done marinating, preheat the oven to 375°F (190°C, or gas mark 5). Line a rimmed baking sheet with aluminum foil or parchment paper, then grease. Drain the wings, place them in a single layer on the baking sheet, then use a pastry brush to lightly coat them with the honey mixture.

Bake for about 40 minutes, or until golden brown and tender, removing the wings from the oven every 10 minutes to brush them with the honey mixture. It will form a thick, sweet glaze.

Sprinkle the wings with the sesame seeds and serve.

◤ **YIELD: 4 SERVINGS**

Light and Fresh Chicken Lettuce Wraps

These lettuce wraps are fun, fresh, and better than takeout because you know exactly what goes into them. No one will even be thinking about the fact that they are low in fat. Most oyster sauces are gluten-free, but be sure to check the label.

1   HEAD ICEBERG LETTUCE

1   TABLESPOON (15 ML) CANOLA OIL

2   CLOVES GARLIC, MINCED

1   TABLESPOON (8 G) FRESHLY GRATED GINGER

1   CUP (70 G) DICED SHIITAKE MUSHROOM CAPS

1½ POUNDS (680 G) GROUND CHICKEN

½   CUP (63 G) CANNED CHOPPED WATER CHESTNUTS, DRAINED AND RINSED

½   CUP (120 ML) OYSTER SAUCE

2   SCALLIONS, SLICED

½   CUP (75 G) FINELY DICED RED BELL PEPPER

    SRIRACHA HOT SAUCE AND CHINESE HOT MUSTARD, FOR SERVING (OPTIONAL)

Cut the iceberg lettuce in half through the stem. Cut off the stem end, then gently separate the lettuce leaves into individual "cups." Rinse under cold water and let drain on paper towels. Set aside.

In a large sauté pan, heat the oil over medium heat. Add the garlic, ginger, and mushrooms, and sauté until fragrant, and the mushrooms have released their juices and are golden, about 5 minutes.

Add the ground chicken and sauté, breaking up the larger pieces until thoroughly cooked, 5 to 7 minutes. Add the water chestnuts and oyster sauce, and stir until well combined.

Transfer the mixture to a platter and garnish with the scallions and bell pepper. Serve with the lettuce cups and sriracha and hot mustard as optional sauces.

❚ YIELD: 6 SERVINGS

+ VARIATION *If you don't have ground chicken, then turkey, beef, pork, or even peeled deveined shrimp would work here. For a vegetarian meal, add crumbled tofu or extra vegetables instead.*

Parmesan Polenta Fries

I love the crispy exterior and creamy center of these cheesy, delicious polenta fries. They pair beautifully with a simple grilled steak for a new twist on the familiar steak frites, or serve them as a starter with a spicy marinara sauce for dipping. Simply omit the cheese for a dairy-free version.

3 CUPS (710 ML) CHICKEN STOCK OR WATER

1 CUP (140 G) YELLOW CORNMEAL, MEDIUM GRIND

¼ CUP (25 G) GRATED PARMESAN CHEESE

SALT AND PEPPER TO TASTE

¼ CUP (32 G) CORNSTARCH

¼ CUP (60 ML) CANOLA OIL, FOR FRYING

CHEF'S TIP *A cast-iron skillet is great for panfrying. Its heavy bottom means no hot spots for even browning!*

Grease a 9 x 9-inch (23 x 23-cm) baking pan and set aside.

Bring the chicken stock to a boil in a medium saucepan. Slowly whisk in the cornmeal to avoid lumps. Cook over medium heat, stirring occasionally, for about 20 minutes, or until very thick, and the polenta doesn't feel gritty when you taste it. Stir in the Parmesan cheese and remove from the heat. Season to taste with salt and pepper.

Pour the polenta into the prepared baking dish, smoothing the top with an offset spatula. Let the polenta sit at room temperature until cooled and firm, about 1 hour.

Place a cutting board on top of the baking pan, then flip the pan over and lift the pan off of the cutting board. Use a sharp knife to cut the polenta into thirds (3-inch [7.5-cm] lengths), then into ½-inch (1.3-cm) sticks. Toss the fries with the cornstarch to lightly coat.

Preheat a heavy-bottomed skilled over medium heat. Add the canola oil, and heat to approximately 375°F (190°C); you can use a candy/deep-fry thermometer if you aren't sure. Panfry the polenta, using tongs to turn the fries occasionally, for 5 to 6 minutes, or until golden and crispy. Transfer to a plate lined with paper towels to drain any excess oil, and serve immediately.

YIELD: 4 SERVINGS

Crispy Tofu with Miso Sauce

Crispy on the outside and soft and creamy on the inside, this tofu recipe will turn even picky eaters into tofu lovers. Miso, which is now carried in most grocery stores, has a fantastically complex flavor, and this sweet and savory sauce is the perfect dip. Chinese five-spice powder is an aromatic seasoning blend of cinnamon, cloves, fennel seed, star anise, and Szechuan pepper—it's optional, but really lovely if you can get it.

FOR MISO SAUCE:

1   CUP (250 G) WHITE MISO

¼   CUP (60 ML) MIRIN

¼   CUP (60 ML) SAKE OR DRY SHERRY

½   CUP (100 G) SUGAR

FOR TOFU:

2   PACKAGES (14 OUNCES, OR 395 G EACH) FIRM TOFU, DRAINED

     CANOLA OIL, FOR FRYING

2   EGG WHITES

¾   CUP (96 G) CORNSTARCH

1   TEASPOON SALT

1   TEASPOON FIVE-SPICE POWDER (OPTIONAL)

To make the sauce: Whisk together the miso, mirin, sake, and sugar in a small saucepan over medium heat. Cook until the sugar is dissolved and the sauce is smooth, about 4 minutes.

To make the tofu: Cut each block of tofu into 6 even slices. Cut each slice corner to corner to make triangles. Place the tofu on several layers of paper towels and top with more paper towels. Press down lightly to remove any excess moisture from the tofu.

Fill a large heavy-bottomed frying pan or cast-iron skillet with 1 inch (2.5 cm) of canola oil. Bring the oil to 350°F (180°C) on a deep-fry thermometer over medium heat.

While the oil is heating, in a small bowl, lightly beat the egg whites. In a medium bowl, combine the cornstarch, salt, and five-spice powder.

Dip each piece of tofu into the egg white, then dredge it in the cornstarch. Carefully place the tofu slices into the hot oil. Fry on each side for about 4 minutes, until lightly golden brown. Serve with the miso sauce.

YIELD: 6 SERVINGS

CHEF'S TIP *Placing the fried tofu on a wire rack instead of paper towels to drain the excess oil will help keep the tofu crisp until ready to serve.*

Pork Satay with Peanut Sauce and Spicy Pickles

This Thai-inspired satay is easy to make and fun to eat. A little planning makes this dish come together in minutes. The day before, marinate the pork and make the pickles, soak the skewers, and make the sauce. The next day, all you have to do is skewer and grill the meat.

FOR SPICY PICKLES:

1   ENGLISH CUCUMBER, SLICED INTO ROUNDS ¼ INCH (6 MM) THICK

2   SHALLOTS, THINLY SLICED

1   CHILE PEPPER, SUCH AS THAI BIRD CHILE, MINCED

¼   CUP (50 G) SUGAR

¼   CUP (60 ML) FRESHLY SQUEEZED LIME JUICE

½   TEASPOON SALT

FOR PORK SATAY:

4   CLOVES GARLIC

1   INCH (2.5-CM) PIECE GINGER, GRATED

4   INCH (10-CM) PIECE LEMON GRASS, ROUGHLY CHOPPED

1   CAN (13.5 OUNCES, OR 400 ML) COCONUT MILK, DIVIDED

1   TEASPOON TURMERIC

2   TABLESPOONS (30 ML) FISH SAUCE

2½ POUNDS (1135 G) BONELESS PORK SHOULDER (PICNIC ROAST)

FOR PEANUT SAUCE:

1   CLOVE GARLIC, MINCED

½   CUP (130 G) PEANUT BUTTER

¼   CUP (60 ML) COCONUT MILK RESERVED FROM THE MARINADE

2   TABLESPOONS (30 G) BROWN SUGAR

1   TABLESPOON (15 ML) FISH SAUCE

2   TABLESPOONS (30 ML) FRESHLY SQUEEZED LIME JUICE

Soak skewers in water for at least 1 hour.

To make the spicy pickles: Toss the cucumber with the shallots, chile, sugar, lime juice, and salt and allow to marinate in the refrigerator for at least 3 hours, or overnight, tossing occasionally.

To make the satay: Make the marinade for the pork by placing the garlic, ginger, and lemon grass in a food processor or blender. Blend until finely chopped. Measure ¼ cup (60 ml) of the coconut milk and set aside for the peanut sauce. Add the remaining coconut milk, turmeric, and fish sauce to the garlic mixture and blend until smooth. Transfer to a large bowl.

Trim the pork of any excess fat. Cut into slices 5 inches (13 cm) long and about ½ inch (1.3 cm) thick and place in the large bowl with the marinade. Toss until combined. Marinate for at least 1 hour or up to overnight.

To make the peanut sauce: Whisk together the garlic, peanut butter, reserved coconut milk, brown sugar, fish sauce, and lime juice in a small bowl. Set aside until ready to use.

Preheat a grill to medium-high. Thread the meat onto the skewers and grill over medium-high heat for 5 to 6 minutes per side, until golden and charred and no longer pink inside. Serve with the pickles and the peanut sauce for dipping.

YIELD: 6 SERVINGS

CHEF'S TIP *The satay can be cooked on the stovetop in a grill pan using the same method as the grill, or it can be made in the oven. Preheat the oven to 450°F (230°C, or gas mark 8) and roast for about 15 minutes.*

Scallion Risotto Cakes

This is the perfect recipe to let your imagination run wild. I like to add chunks of ham, peas, or diced artichoke hearts for easy and delicious variations. The potato-chip crumb coating browns beautifully in the oven, so there's no need to panfry.

1   CUP (195 G) ARBORIO RICE

1½ CUPS (355 ML) CHICKEN STOCK

    SALT AND PEPPER TO TASTE

1   BUNCH SCALLIONS (6 TO 8 SCALLIONS)

½   CUP (50 G) GRATED PARMESAN CHEESE

2   LARGE EGGS, SEPARATED

4   OUNCES (115 G) POTATO CHIPS, FINELY
    CRUSHED (ABOUT 2 CUPS [115 G])

✖ CHEF'S TIP *These are the perfect side dish, but I love to make them bite-size and serve them at cocktail parties, too. Prepare them up to 12 hours in advance, to the point that they are coated in potato chip crumbs. Cover and refrigerate, then toss them in the oven right before your guests arrive. You'll make it look effortless, and they will think you're a culinary genius.*

Preheat the oven to 375°F (190°C, or gas mark 5).

In medium heavy saucepan, combine the rice and stock, and salt to taste. Bring to a boil over high heat, then reduce the heat to low and simmer, covered, until the rice is tender and the chicken stock has been absorbed, about 20 minutes.

Meanwhile, bring a small saucepan of water to a boil. Fill a small bowl with ice water. Cut the green tops off of the scallions, and blanch them in the boiling water, about 2 to 3 minutes, then drain and shock them in the bowl of ice water. Pat the blanched scallion greens dry, and finely mince them. Thinly slice the white parts of the scallions.

Combine the cooked rice, scallions, Parmesan, and egg yolks in a large bowl. Season to taste with salt and pepper. Refrigerate the mixture until cool enough to handle, 15 to 20 minutes.

Form the rice mixture into eight 3-inch (7.5-cm) patties, carefully pressing the mixture together just firmly enough to hold without making the risotto cakes too dense.

Place the egg whites and crushed potato chips in separate bowls. Dredge each risotto cake in the egg white, letting the excess drip off, then in the crushed potato chips and transfer to a baking sheet.

Bake for about 10 minutes, or until crispy and golden on the bottom, then flip and cook another 5 minutes for even browning. Transfer to a plate and serve immediately.

◪ YIELD: 8 RISOTTO CAKES

Prosciutto-Stuffed Figs with Arugula Oil

Sweet figs and salty prosciutto are a match made in heaven. Peppery arugula oil drizzled over the figs makes the perfect contrast. This is an easy make-ahead appetizer. Stuff the figs and make the arugula oil the day before and store in the refrigerator. To serve, just bring to room temperature and drizzle with the oil.

FOR ARUGULA OIL:

½   **CUP (10 G) PACKED ARUGULA LEAVES**

½   **CUP (120 ML) EXTRA-VIRGIN OLIVE OIL**
    SALT AND PEPPER TO TASTE

FOR FIGS:

12   **FRESH FIGS**

12   **THIN SLICES PROSCIUTTO DI PARMA OR PROSCIUTTO DI SAN DANIELE**

To make the arugula oil: Place the arugula, extra-virgin olive oil, and salt and pepper in a food processor or blender. Process until smooth. Transfer to a small airtight container, and chill in the refrigerator for about an hour. Pour the oil through a fine-mesh strainer to remove any pulp from the arugula but leave its wonderful flavor in the olive oil.

To make the figs: Slice off the stem of each fig and cut an X into the top, about halfway down the fig. Use your fingers to open up the fig and season the inside with salt and pepper. Fold 1 slice of prosciutto into a fan shape and stuff it into a fig. Repeat for all the figs. Drizzle with the arugula oil and serve.

▧ YIELD: 12 FIGS

➕ VARIATION *If fresh figs aren't available, try this recipe with dried figs. Instead of stuffing the fresh figs, wrap the dried figs with prosciutto and bake in a 375°F (190°C, or gas mark 5) oven for about 10 minutes to soften the figs and heat them through. Drizzle with the arugula oil and serve.*

Bacon-Wrapped Dates with Lemon Aioli

I serve these at every single cocktail party I have. There's something completely perfect about a sweet date wrapped in crispy, salty bacon served with a dollop of lemony mayo and a crunchy endive leaf. You won't regret it if you decide to make a double batch!

12 SLICES BACON (REGULAR, NOT THICK CUT)

24 DATES, PITTED

1 CLOVE GARLIC

½ CUP (115 G) MAYONNAISE

1 TEASPOON LEMON ZEST

1 TABLESPOON (15 ML) FRESH LEMON JUICE

24 BELGIAN ENDIVE LEAVES, WASHED AND TRIMMED

Preheat the oven to 350°F (180°C, or gas mark 4).

Cut the slices of bacon in half. Wrap each date in a half slice of bacon and place on a baking sheet, seam side down. Bake for 20 to 25 minutes, or until the bacon is crisp.

Meanwhile, make the aioli by placing the garlic clove in a food processor or mini food processor. Pulse to finely chop the garlic, then add the mayonnaise, lemon zest, and lemon juice. Process until well combined.

Assemble the dish by placing the endive leaves on a serving platter. Place one bacon-wrapped date on each leaf, then top with a teaspoon of the lemon aioli. Serve warm or at room temperature.

YIELD: 24 DATES

 CHEF'S TIP *Make a lighter version of this recipe by using turkey bacon and reduced-fat mayonnaise in the aioli.*

Shrimp Summer Rolls

These are a great warm weather treat. They require very little cooking and are full of hydrating, crisp vegetables. Look for cellophane noodles and spring roll papers at your nearest Asian grocery.

24	PEELED, DEVEINED SHRIMP
2	OUNCES (56 G) CELLOPHANE (BEAN THREAD) NOODLES
12	DRIED RICE PAPER SPRING ROLL SKINS
1	MANGO, PEELED, PITTED, AND CUT INTO 12 SLICES
1½	CUPS (75 G) BEAN SPROUTS
1½	CUPS (165 G) SHREDDED CARROT
1½	CUPS (83 G) SHREDDED RED LEAF OR ICEBERG LETTUCE
12	SPRIGS CILANTRO
12	BASIL LEAVES
1	CUP (275 G) SWEET CHILI SAUCE

CHEF'S TIP *These are best served the same day but may be made a couple of hours in advance. Store in an airtight container with plastic wrap separating each roll so that they don't stick together and rip the rice paper.*

Fill a large stockpot with cold water and enough salt to make it taste like seawater. Cover and bring to a boil. Fill a large mixing bowl with ice and water. Add the shrimp to the boiling water and allow to cook for 3 minutes, or until just cooked through. Pour the shrimp into a colander to drain and add the shrimp to the cold ice water to stop the cooking and cool the shrimp. Drain again, remove the tails, and slice the shrimp in half lengthwise. Set aside.

Fill a medium pot with cold water and enough salt to make it taste like seawater. Cover and bring to a boil. Add the cellophane noodles, remove from the heat, and allow to sit, covered, for 10 minutes, or until tender and completely translucent. Drain the noodles, and set aside to cool.

Place about 1 inch (2.5 cm) of hot water in a bowl or rimmed baking dish large enough for the rice paper wrappers to fit in. Lay out all of the prepared ingredients before beginning to make the wraps.

Start by dipping the rice paper in the hot water until completely softened and pliable, about 15 seconds. Lay out on a large cutting board or clean countertop. Place 4 slices of shrimp with the pink side down on the lower third of the rice paper. On top of that, place a small amount of noodles, mango, bean sprouts, carrot, lettuce, 1 cilantro sprig, and 1 basil leaf. Start to roll the bottom of the paper up and around the filling. Then fold in the sides, one at a time, and continue to roll away from you. The rice paper will be slightly sticky and flexible and will make a nice tight roll that seals itself. Repeat with the remaining ingredients until you have 12 summer rolls.

Serve with the sweet chili sauce on the side for dipping.

YIELD: 12 ROLLS

Roasted Cauliflower with Red Pepper Hummus

This recipe is quick and simple to put together when you use canned chickpeas, but if you have time, cook the beans yourself for even better flavor. The red pepper adds a touch of sweetness and beautiful color to a classic hummus. Simple roasted cauliflower is perfect for dipping.

1   RED BELL PEPPER

1   TEASPOON PLUS 1 TABLESPOON (15 ML) OLIVE OIL, DIVIDED

1   HEAD CAULIFLOWER, CUT INTO LARGE FLORETS

    SALT AND PEPPER TO TASTE

1   CLOVE GARLIC

1½ CUPS (375 G) COOKED CHICKPEAS OR 1 CAN (15.5 OUNCES, OR 430 G)

¼   CUP (60 ML) EXTRA-VIRGIN OLIVE OIL

1   TEASPOON TAHINI

2   TEASPOONS LEMON JUICE

1   TABLESPOON (15 ML) WATER

> ✗ **CHEF'S TIP** *For silky smooth hummus, use your fingers to pop the chickpeas out of their skins before puréeing. It's extra work, but the texture is perfection!*

Preheat the oven to 400°F (200°C, or gas mark 6). Place the whole bell pepper on a baking sheet and rub with 1 teaspoon (5 ml) of the olive oil. Place the baking sheet in the oven and roast the pepper for 20 to 25 minutes, turning occasionally, until the skin is black and blistered. Remove the pepper from the oven and let cool.

Place the cauliflower florets on a separate baking sheet. Toss with the remaining 1 tablespoon (15 ml) olive oil, season with salt and pepper, and roast for 20 to 25 minutes, or until tender and the edges of the cauliflower begin to turn brown and slightly crisp. Set aside.

When the pepper is cool enough to handle, use your fingers to peel away the skin from the pepper, and remove the stem and seeds.

Place the clove of garlic in the bowl of a food processor and pulse to chop. Add the peeled and deseeded roasted pepper, chickpeas, extra-virgin olive oil, tahini, lemon juice, and water and process until very smooth and creamy. Season to taste with salt and pepper, and serve with the roasted cauliflower for dipping.

🔪 **YIELD: 6 SERVINGS**

Sweet Mango Guacamole

This guacamole has the unexpected addition of sweet, ripe mango. Tortilla chips or veggies make a great accompaniment, but I love to fold guacamole into soft corn tortillas, sprinkle with hot sauce, and devour!

2   RIPE AVOCADOS

1   CUP (175 G) DICED MANGO

½   CUP (80 G) DICED RED ONION

½   CUP (90 G) DICED SEEDED TOMATO

1   TABLESPOON (9 G) MINCED JALAPEÑO OR SERRANO PEPPER

2   TABLESPOONS (2 G) CHOPPED CILANTRO

1   TABLESPOON (15 ML) LIME JUICE

      SALT AND PEPPER TO TASTE

Use a chef's knife to cut the avocados in half lengthwise, sliding the knife along the pit in the center of the avocado. Twist the halves to separate them. Use a spoon to gently scoop the pit out of the avocado and discard. Use the spoon to separate the thick skin from the avocado flesh by running it along the edge between the two.

Dice the avocados and place them in a bowl. Add the mango, red onion, tomato, jalapeño, cilantro, lime juice, and a sprinkle of salt and pepper to the bowl. Stir to combine, then serve.

YIELD: 6 SERVINGS

Spicy Queso with Chorizo

Hard, cured chorizo sausage is typically found in Spain, while fresh, uncooked chorizo is Mexican. This creamy, meaty, and spicy cheese sauce calls for fresh (Mexican) chorizo, but if finely diced, the cured kind would work, too!

8   OUNCES (225 G) FRESH CHORIZO SAUSAGE

½   CUP (115 G) CREAM CHEESE

1   CUP (235 ML) MILK

¼   CUP (65 G) SALSA

12   OUNCES (340 G) SHREDDED PEPPER JACK CHEESE

1   TABLESPOON (8 G) CORNSTARCH

Using a small, sharp knife, slice the sausage casing lengthwise and squeeze out the meat inside. Discard the casing. In a large skillet over medium heat, cook the sausage, breaking up the big pieces and stirring to cook evenly, until golden brown, 5 to 8 minutes.

Decrease the heat to low, add the cream cheese, milk, and salsa, and stir until combined. In a medium bowl, toss the pepper Jack cheese with the cornstarch until evenly coated. Add to the chorizo mixture a handful at a time and cook until completely melted and smooth.

YIELD: 6 SERVINGS

Gorgonzola Fondue

The national dish of Switzerland, fondue is a melted cheese sauce served in a shared pot into which you dip items skewered onto a long fork. One of the best and most memorable fondues I've had was high in the Swiss Alps. This version with Gorgonzola has an incredibly complex flavor.

1¼ CUPS (300 ML) WHITE WINE

1   SHALLOT, MINCED

1   POUND (455 G) GORGONZOLA, CRUMBLED

1   POUND (455 G) AGED WHITE CHEDDAR, SHREDDED

¼   CUP (32 G) CORNSTARCH

> ✗ **CHEF'S TIP** *Lots of different varieties of cheese could be substituted for the Gorgonzola and Cheddar in this recipe. Try it with your favorite high quality cheeses.*

In a fondue pot over low heat, combine the white wine and shallot. Bring to a simmer. In a medium bowl, combine the cheeses and cornstarch. Toss until evenly coated. Add the cheeses to the wine a handful at a time while continuously stirring. Cook for about 5 minutes, or until the mixture is smooth and creamy.

Arrange a variety of foods to be dipped on a platter or in small bowls. You can dip just about anything in cheese! I love to serve this with potato or tortilla chips, cherry tomatoes, baby carrots, cucumber, apples, boiled baby potatoes, and bits of sausage or chicken.

Serve the fondue in the fondue pot in the center of the table using the fondue pot warmer to keep it warm. (If you don't have a fondue pot, use a heavy-bottomed saucepan. If the fondue becomes too cool on the table, warm the pot over low heat.)

◼ YIELD: 8 SERVINGS

Honey Nut Trail Mix Bars

These are my go-to bar for a nutritious breakfast on the run or a portable snack.
They are infinitely better than the packaged kind you buy at the store and are simple to make.
Feel free to experiment with different dried fruit and nut combinations.

1½ CUPS (40 G) CRISPY BROWN RICE CEREAL

½ CUP (75 G) WHOLE CASHEWS

½ CUP (70 G) WHOLE ALMONDS

½ CUP (75 G) ROASTED SHELLED PISTACHIOS

½ CUP (50 G) WHOLE PECANS OR WALNUTS

½ CUP (75 G) RAISINS

½ CUP (60 G) DRIED CRANBERRIES

¼ CUP (36 G) SESAME SEEDS

¼ CUP (28 G) FLAXSEED MEAL

¼ CUP (20 G) FLAKED COCONUT

½ CUP (170 G) HONEY

¼ CUP (60 G) FIRMLY PACKED BROWN SUGAR

¼ TEASPOON SALT

2 TABLESPOONS (16 G) CORNSTARCH

CHEF'S TIP *Flax is a great source of fiber and omega-3 fatty acids, but whole flaxseed cannot be digested by the body. Be sure to buy ground flaxseed or grind your own in a clean coffee grinder!*
■ *For a little decadence, drizzle or dip these in melted dark chocolate.*

Preheat the oven to 300°F (150°C, or gas mark 2). Cut a 9 x 9-inch (23 x 23-cm) piece of parchment paper. Grease a 9 x 9-inch (23 x 23-cm) baking pan, line with the parchment paper, grease the paper, and set aside.

In a large mixing bowl, combine the brown rice cereal, cashews, almonds, pistachios, pecans, raisins, dried cranberries, sesame seeds, flaxseed meal, and flaked coconut. Set aside.

In a medium saucepan, combine the honey, brown sugar, salt, and cornstarch. Bring to a gentle boil over medium heat. Pour the mixture over the dry ingredients and toss until evenly coated.

Transfer the mixture to the prepared pan. Use another piece of parchment paper to press down the mixture so that it is flat and evenly distributed to the corners of the pan. Remove top layer of parchment and bake for 30 minutes. Let cool completely in the pan, several hours.

Turn the mixture out onto a cutting board, peeling away the parchment paper on the bottom. Using a serrated knife, cut into 16 squares. Store in a zipper-top bag or an airtight container at room temperature for about a week.

▧ YIELD: 16 BARS

Stovetop Cinnamon Kettle Corn

I have the fondest memories of going to the country fair and waiting in line for what seemed like forever for a huge bag full of salty and sweet kettle corn. I loved watching them pop it in a humongous copper kettle and stir it with a giant paddle. My easy version has a touch of cinnamon, but leave it out if you prefer.

⅓ CUP (70 G) SUGAR

¼ TEASPOON GROUND CINNAMON

3 TABLESPOONS (45 ML) CANOLA OIL

½ CUP (65 G) POPCORN KERNELS

1 TEASPOON SALT

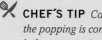 **CHEF'S TIP** *Careful! Make sure the popping is completely stopped before uncovering the pot.*

Combine the sugar and cinnamon in a small bowl and set aside.

Heat a large, heavy-bottomed pot with a well-fitting lid over high heat. Add the canola oil and 3 popcorn kernels. Cover the pot and wait for them to pop.

When you've heard all 3 kernels pop, your pot is hot enough to make your kettle corn. Add the remaining popcorn kernels and the sugar mixture to the pot, and give it a good stir with a silicone spatula. Cover the pot and shake until the kernels begin to pop.

Decrease the heat to medium-high, and continue to shake the pot as the popcorn pops. When the popping slows to every 3 to 4 seconds, remove the pot from the heat and carefully transfer the popcorn to a large bowl. Sprinkle with the salt and toss to coat all of the kernels. Let cool, then store in a gallon-size zipper-top bag for up to 1 week.

◼ **YIELD: 10 CUPS (200 G)**

Chapter

6

simply **SATISFYING**
SALADS *and* **SOUPS**

Lobster Cobb Salad

The addition of lobster, mango, and goat cheese to the traditional cobb salad makes this salad vibrate with color and flavor. This salad is best served on a platter or a wide shallow bowl to show off all the beautiful ingredients.

1 POUND (455-G) LOBSTER TAIL

2 TABLESPOONS (28 G) UNSALTED BUTTER

1 CLOVE GARLIC, SLICED

SALT AND PEPPER TO TASTE

8 CUPS (440 G) CHOPPED ROMAINE LETTUCE

1 AVOCADO, PEELED, SEEDED, AND DICED

4 HARD-BOILED EGGS, PEELED AND CHOPPED

1 CUP (120 G) DICED CUCUMBER

1 CUP (150 G) CHERRY TOMATOES, HALVED

1 MANGO, PEELED, SEEDED, AND DICED

4 OUNCES (115 G) GOAT CHEESE, CRUMBLED

4 SLICES COOKED BACON, CRUMBLED

½ CUP (120 ML) PERFECT BALSAMIC VINAIGRETTE (PAGE 126)

Preheat the oven to 350°F (180°C, or gas mark 4).

Prepare the lobster tail by cutting down the length of the underside of the tail with scissors. Use your hands to split the shell along the incision and remove the meat from the shell. In a medium oven-proof sauté pan, heat the butter and garlic over medium heat. Cook for 1 to 2 minutes, until fragrant. Season the lobster meat with salt and pepper and add it to the pan. Sear each side for about 1 minute. Transfer the pan to the oven and bake for about 5 minutes, or until the lobster is opaque and firm. Remove the lobster from the hot pan and set aside to cool. Once the lobster has cooled, slice it into bite-size pieces.

Assemble the salad on a large platter. First, spread the romaine lettuce as the base of the salad. Starting in the center, place the lobster, avocado, eggs, cucumber, tomatoes, mango, goat cheese, and bacon in individual rows going across the entire salad. Serve with the balsamic vinaigrette on the side.

YIELD: 4 SERVINGS

CHEF'S TIP *The best lobster tails are from cold waters; they have a superior taste and tender texture. For convenience, you can buy frozen lobster tails. Just defrost in the refrigerator for 24 hours before cooking.*

Black and Bleu Salad

I use English Stilton in this recipe, but Italian Gorgonzola, French Roquefort,
or any of your favorite bleu cheeses would all work well here. This dressing also makes the perfect dip
for the Parmesan Polenta Fries on page 94.

1   CLOVE GARLIC

½   CUP (60 G) CRUMBLED BLEU CHEESE,
    DIVIDED

1   CUP (225 G) MAYONNAISE

1   TEASPOON TABASCO SAUCE

¼   CUP (60 ML) WELL-SHAKEN BUTTERMILK

¼   TEASPOON FRESHLY CRACKED BLACK
    PEPPER

2   POUNDS (910 G) FLANK STEAK
    SALT AND PEPPER TO TASTE

12 CUPS (660 G) BABY SPINACH LEAVES

1   CUP (150 G) CHERRY TOMATOES, HALVED

1   BELL PEPPER, STEMMED, SEEDED,
    AND SLICED

1   CUP (120 G) SEEDLESS CUCUMBER
    SLICES

¼   CUP (34 G) PINE NUTS OR CHOPPED
    WALNUTS

To make the dressing: Place the garlic clove in the bowl of a food processor (a mini food processor works well here). Pulse to finely chop. Add ¼ cup (30 g) of the blue cheese, the mayonnaise, Tabasco, buttermilk, and black pepper to the food processor and process until smooth. Transfer the mixture to a bowl, and stir in the remaining ¼ cup (30 g) bleu cheese. Set aside while you make the salad.

To make the salad: Season the flank steak generously with salt and pepper. Preheat a grill, grill pan, or broiler on high, then cook the steak for 3 to 4 minutes per side for medium-rare. Transfer to a plate and let rest while you assemble the salads.

Place the baby spinach on 6 plates or 1 large platter. Arrange the tomatoes, bell pepper, cucumber, and nuts over the spinach. Drizzle with the bleu cheese dressing.

Thinly slice the steak against the grain of the meat, and arrange over the salads. Serve while the steak is still warm.

YIELD: 6 SERVINGS

CHEF'S TIP *This is a great way to use up any leftover steak you may have in the refrigerator!*

Quinoa Salad with Roasted Chicken, Apricots, and Goat Cheese

Quinoa is a nutritional powerhouse, full of nutrients, fiber, and protein. This is my favorite way to eat quinoa, and I make some variation on this salad every week (e.g., with sweet potatoes, cranberries, and pecans in fall, or roasted red peppers, raisins, and pine nuts in winter). It's filling and flavorful and holds well if you want to make it a day or two in advance. I serve mine at room temperature or chilled.

2   TEASPOONS OLIVE OIL

1   POUND (455 G) BONELESS, SKINLESS CHICKEN BREAST OR THIGHS

    SALT AND PEPPER TO TASTE

1½ CUPS (260 G) QUINOA, RINSED

2   CUPS (470 ML) WATER

½   CUP (65 G) DRIED APRICOTS, CHOPPED

4   SCALLIONS, THINLY SLICED

¾   CUP (85 G) SLICED ALMONDS, TOASTED

2   CLOVES GARLIC, MINCED

1   TEASPOON HONEY

1   TEASPOON DIJON MUSTARD

2   TABLESPOONS (30 ML) WHITE WINE VINEGAR

2   TABLESPOONS (30 ML) EXTRA-VIRGIN OLIVE OIL

4   CUPS (220 G) MIXED BABY GREENS

4   OUNCES (115 G) GOAT CHEESE, CRUMBLED

✗ CHEF'S TIP *Searing the chicken on the stovetop to brown it, then finishing it in the oven with a slower, gentler heat will keep the chicken moist and flavorful. Just make sure your sauté pan is oven-safe.*

Preheat the oven to 350°F (180°C, or gas mark 4).

Heat an oven-safe sauté pan over medium-high heat. Add the olive oil to the pan. Season the chicken with salt and pepper and sear in the olive oil for 3 to 4 minutes on one side, until golden. Flip over the chicken pieces, and then transfer the pan to the oven and bake for 5 to 6 minutes for chicken breast, or 7 to 8 minutes if you are using boneless skinless thighs. Remove from the oven and set aside.

Meanwhile, in a large saucepan, combine the rinsed quinoa and water. Bring to a boil over high heat, then decrease the heat to medium-low. Simmer for 15 minutes, or until the germ uncurls from the seed and the quinoa is tender and the water is absorbed. Transfer the quinoa to a large bowl, and let it cool.

Thinly slice the chicken and add it to the bowl with the quinoa. Add the apricots, scallions, almonds, and garlic to the bowl.

In a separate small bowl, whisk together the honey, Dijon, and vinegar. Continuing to whisk, slowly drizzle in the extra-virgin olive oil to make a vinaigrette. Add the vinaigrette to the quinoa, season the salad with salt and pepper, and toss to combine.

Place 1 cup (55 g) of the mixed greens on each of 4 plates, divide the quinoa salad evenly among the plates, and top with 1 ounce (28 g) of the crumbled goat cheese.

▧ YIELD: 4 SERVINGS

Roasted Beet, Pistachio, and Feta Salad

*Incredibly sweet and earthy, roasted beets are simple to make and packed with nutrients.
If you buy beets with the greens still attached, do not discard them. Beet greens are super healthy on
their own and can be substituted for other greens, such as spinach, kale, and collards.*

1	POUND (455 G) BEETS
1	SHALLOT, FINELY MINCED
½	CUP (75 G) ROASTED SHELLED PISTACHIOS
½	CUP (75 G) CRUMBLED FETA
2	TABLESPOONS (30 ML) EXTRA-VIRGIN OLIVE OIL OR WALNUT OIL
4	TEASPOONS (20 ML) WHITE WINE VINEGAR
	SALT AND PEPPER TO TASTE

✖ **CHEF'S TIP** *Keep your fingers from turning pink by using disposable gloves to handle the beets!*

Preheat the oven to 400°F (200°C, or gas mark 6).

Wash the beets to clean off the dirt and remove the beet greens if they are still attached. Wrap the beets loosely in aluminum foil, then seal tightly to lock in the steam. Place on a baking sheet and roast for 1 hour. For small beets you may reduce the roasting time slightly, and for larger ones you may need to increase it. The beets should be tender, easily pierced with the tip of a knife. Remove from the foil and set aside to cool slightly.

When cool enough to handle, peel the beets by rubbing off the skins with your fingers. They should remove easily, but use a paring knife if you have any trouble. Cut off the rough end where the greens were attached. Cut the beets into bite-size pieces.

In a large mixing bowl, combine the beets, shallot, pistachios, feta, extra-virgin olive oil, and white wine vinegar. Season with salt and pepper, and toss to combine.

◗ **YIELD: 4 SERVINGS**

➕ **VARIATION** *If you don't have time to roast the beets or want to try something different, try this recipe using raw beets. Raw beets are delicious and have a great crunch. Peel the beets with a vegetable peeler and then shred them either by hand or with a food processor. Follow the remaining steps in the recipe as directed.*

Crab and Corn Salad with Lime Vinaigrette

This salad is best in the summer when fresh, sweet corn is available. People are always surprised when I serve salads like this with raw corn right off of the cob, but it is crisp, sweet, and delicious without any cooking. Of course, you can use thawed frozen corn if fresh is not available.

1   POUND (455 G) CRABMEAT, PICKED THROUGH FOR SHELL FRAGMENTS

2   CUPS (300 G) CORN KERNELS (ABOUT 3 EARS OF CORN)

1   CUP (150 G) DICED RED BELL PEPPER

4   SCALLIONS, WHITE AND GREEN PARTS, THINLY SLICED

1   JALAPEÑO PEPPER, SEEDED AND MINCED

2   TABLESPOONS (2 G) CHOPPED CILANTRO

1   TEASPOON LIME ZEST

¼   CUP (60 ML) FRESHLY SQUEEZED LIME JUICE

1   TABLESPOON (15 G) DIJON MUSTARD

1   TABLESPOON (20 G) HONEY

2   TABLESPOONS (30 ML) OLIVE OIL

    SALT AND PEPPER TO TASTE

2   HEADS BUTTER LETTUCE, LEAVES SEPARATED, WASHED, AND PATTED DRY

Combine the crabmeat, corn, bell pepper, scallions, jalapeño, cilantro, and lime zest in a large bowl. Set aside.

In a small bowl, whisk together the lime juice, Dijon, honey, and olive oil to make a dressing. Pour the dressing over the crab mixture, season to taste with salt and pepper, then stir to combine.

Arrange the butter lettuce on 6 plates or a large platter. Spoon the crab salad over the lettuce leaves and serve.

YIELD: 6 SERVINGS

CHEF'S TIP *Jumbo lump crab is the most desirable crabmeat because it is large, succulent pieces of crab. It's also the most expensive. Lump or claw meat is less expensive, and both work well here. Use what works for your budget!*

Creamy and Colorful Raw Kale Salad

Kale is one of those super-healthy foods people seem to turn their noses up at.
This salad is fresh, crunchy, and healthy, but most importantly, it tastes fantastic!

1	CLOVE GARLIC
2	AVOCADOS, PEELED AND PITTED
¼	CUP (60 ML) FRESHLY SQUEEZED LEMON JUICE
2	TABLESPOONS (30 ML) WATER
	SALT AND PEPPER TO TASTE
1	BUNCH KALE, STEMS REMOVED, CHOPPED INTO BITE-SIZE PIECES
1	CUP (110 G) GRATED CARROT
½	CUP (40 G) PUMPKIN SEEDS, RAW
1	APPLE, CORED AND DICED

Place the clove of garlic in a food processor (a mini food processor works well here) and pulse to chop. Add the avocados, lemon juice, water, and a sprinkle of salt and pepper to the food processor, then process until the mixture is very smooth and creamy.

Place the kale, carrot, pumpkin seeds, and apple into a large bowl. Add the avocado dressing to the salad, then use tongs to toss the kale until the dressing coats all of the leaves evenly. Cover the bowl with plastic wrap and let it sit in the refrigerator to marinate for at least 20 minutes before serving.

YIELD: 4 SERVINGS

CHEF'S TIP *You can serve this salad right away, but letting it sit with the acidic dressing on it softens and tenderizes the kale for an even better texture!*

Crispy Duck Salad with Shredded Vegetables

Duck is such a decadent and delicious meat to cook with. Here, its richness is contrasted by piles of fresh shredded veggies and a tangy, oil-free dressing, resulting in an ultra-refreshing and surprisingly light salad. If you've never cooked with duck before, this is a great place to try it; it's easy! Of course, you can use chicken breast if you prefer, and it's also great meat-free.

2   TABLESPOONS (30 ML) FRESH LIME JUICE

2   TABLESPOONS (30 ML) FISH SAUCE

1   TEASPOON MINCED CHILE PEPPER, SUCH AS THAI BIRD OR SERRANO

1   TABLESPOON (15 G) BROWN SUGAR

2   DUCK BREASTS (6 OUNCES, OR 170 G EACH)

     SALT AND PEPPER TO TASTE

2   CUPS (60 G) WATERCRESS OR BABY SPINACH

1   CUP (75 G) JULIENNED SNOW PEAS

1   CUP (50 G) BEAN SPROUTS

1   CUP (150 G) JULIENNED RED BELL PEPPER

1   CUP (160 G) JULIENNED RED ONION

1   CUP (165 G) JULIENNED MANGO

¼   CUP (4 G) CHOPPED CILANTRO

¼   CUP (35 G) CHOPPED PEANUTS

In a small bowl, combine the lime juice, fish sauce, minced chile, and brown sugar. Whisk until the sugar is dissolved. Set aside.

Use your fingers to peel the thick layer of fatty skin off of the duck breasts. Season the duck breasts and the skin with salt and pepper. Slice the skin of the duck into strips ¼ inch (6 mm) thick.

Heat a medium sauté pan over medium-high heat. Add the duck skin to the pan, and cook until the fat is rendered and the skin becomes crispy, like bacon. Transfer to a plate lined with paper towels to absorb any excess fat.

Pour most of the remaining fat out of the sauté pan (except for about 1 teaspoon) and discard. Add the duck breasts to the pan and sear for 3 to 4 minutes per side for medium-rare or longer for your desired doneness. Transfer the duck to a plate to rest.

In a large bowl, combine the watercress, snow peas, bean sprouts, bell pepper, red onion, mango, cilantro, and peanuts. Thinly slice the duck breast and add it to the bowl. Drizzle with the dressing and use tongs to toss all of the ingredients together and evenly coat them in the dressing.

Arrange the salad on 4 plates or a large platter, and garnish with the crispy duck skin. Serve immediately.

◾ YIELD: 4 SERVINGS

✕ **CHEF'S TIP** *Although duck is poultry, it's considered a red meat and the breast is typically served medium-rare like a steak.*

Bistro Chicken Salad

Gently poaching the chicken breast in the oven makes the meat tender and juicy without added fat. The crunch from the pecans and the sweetness from the cranberries give this dish great texture and flavor. I serve this over baby greens for a great salad, or in romaine lettuce leaves as lettuce wraps.

1½ **POUNDS (680 G) BONELESS, SKINLESS CHICKEN BREAST**

2   **CUPS (470 ML) CHICKEN STOCK OR WATER**

1   **BAY LEAF**

¼   **CUP (60 G) MAYONNAISE**

1   **TABLESPOON (15 G) DIJON MUSTARD**

1   **TABLESPOON (15 ML) LEMON JUICE**

1   **TABLESPOON CHOPPED FRESH (4 G) CHERVIL OR TARRAGON**

1   **SHALLOT, MINCED**

¼   **CUP (30 G) DRIED CRANBERRIES**

¼   **CUP (28 G) CHOPPED PECANS, TOASTED**

SALT AND PEPPER TO TASTE

Preheat the oven to 350°F (180°C, or gas mark 4).

Place the chicken breast in a baking dish, pour the stock over the chicken, and add the bay leaf. Cover the pan tightly with aluminum foil and bake for about 25 to 30 minutes, or until cooked through and tender.

While the chicken is poaching in the oven, make the dressing. In a medium bowl, combine the mayonnaise, mustard, lemon juice, chervil, and minced shallot. Set aside.

When the chicken is fully cooked, remove the chicken breast from the poaching liquid and allow to cool to room temperature. Cut the chicken into a small bite-size chunks and toss with the dressing, dried cranberries, and pecans until well combined. Season to taste with salt and pepper and serve.

◪ YIELD: 6 SERVINGS

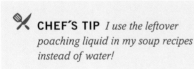 **CHEF'S TIP** *I use the leftover poaching liquid in my soup recipes instead of water!*

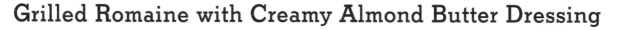

Grilled Romaine with Creamy Almond Butter Dressing

I love this salad because it's delicious and unexpected. The dressing is thick and creamy, and complements the tender grilled romaine perfectly.

1   CLOVE GARLIC, MINCED

½   CUP (130 G) SMOOTH ALMOND BUTTER

½   CUP (115 G) MAYONNAISE

2   TABLESPOONS (30 ML) WHITE WINE VINEGAR

½   CUP (120 ML) WARM WATER

    SALT AND PEPPER TO TASTE

3   ROMAINE HEARTS

1   TABLESPOON (15 ML) EXTRA-VIRGIN OLIVE OIL

2   TABLESPOONS (18 G) CHOPPED ALMONDS, FOR GARNISH

+ VARIATION *Substitute vegan mayonnaise for a completely vegan version of this salad.*

In a small bowl, whisk together the garlic, almond butter, mayonnaise, white wine vinegar, and warm water until smooth and homogeneous. Season to taste with salt and pepper. Set the dressing aside while you grill the romaine.

Cut the romaine hearts in half lengthwise. Leave the stem intact to hold the lettuce leaves together while you grill, but trim off the very end where it has turned brown. Brush the romaine hearts lightly with the olive oil and season with salt and pepper.

Preheat a grill or grill pan over medium-high heat. Grill the romaine for about 6 minutes, turning once so that the leaves begin to char but the lettuce doesn't become mushy.

Place the grilled romaine on a plate, cut side up, and drizzle with the almond butter dressing. Garnish with the chopped almonds and serve.

Any leftover dressing will keep in the fridge for up to a week; bring it to room temperature before serving because it will get thick when chilled.

YIELD: 6 SERVINGS

Simple Greens with Perfect Balsamic Vinaigrette

Have you ever wondered how to make a smooth, thick vinaigrette that doesn't separate?
This foolproof recipe is it! Traditionally, vinaigrettes have a 3:1 oil to vinegar ratio, but I'm all about
breaking the rules. This one is a little lighter, but still not too tangy. Make it ahead of time and store
it in the refrigerator to make salad preparation quick and easy.

FOR PERFECT BALSAMIC VINAIGRETTE:

½   CUP (120 ML) BALSAMIC VINEGAR

2   TABLESPOONS (40 G) HONEY

3   TABLESPOONS (40 G) DIJON MUSTARD
    SALT AND PEPPER TO TASTE

¾   CUP (180 ML) EXTRA-VIRGIN OLIVE OIL

FOR GREENS:

2   CUPS (110 G) BABY GREENS PER PERSON

To make the dressing: In a medium mixing bowl, combine the balsamic vinegar, honey, Dijon, and a pinch of salt and pepper. Whisk until combined. Slowly pour in the oil while constantly whisking until thoroughly incorporated. Season again with salt and pepper if needed. Store in jar or bottle in the fridge for up to a week.

To make the greens: Place the desired amount of baby greens in a large mixing bowl. Drizzle with a small amount of dressing and a pinch of salt and pepper. Toss with tongs to coat all of the lettuce with a light coating of the dressing. Serve right away.

YIELD: 1½ CUPS (355 ML) DRESSING

CHEF'S TIP *For a quicker method of making vinaigrette, just combine all the ingredients in a mason jar or glass bottle. Seal tightly, then shake well until the dressing is smooth and emulsified.*

VARIATION *Substitute apple cider vinegar, red or white wine vinegar, or grapeseed or walnut oil for easy variations on this vinaigrette.*

Home-style Split Pea Soup

This split pea soup is simple to make with basic ingredients that you probably already have on hand.
You could use green or yellow peas here. Dried peas are full of fiber and protein and are low in calories.

2   SLICES BACON, DICED

1   ONION, DICED

1   CUP (130 G) DICED CARROT

1   CUP (120 G) DICED CELERY

2   CUPS (450 G) SPLIT PEAS, PICKED OVER
    AND RINSED

6   CUPS (1410 ML) WATER

4   CUPS (940 ML) CHICKEN OR VEGETABLE
    STOCK

1   BAY LEAF

2   TEASPOONS LEMON ZEST

1   TABLESPOON (15 ML) LEMON JUICE
    SALT AND PEPPER TO TASTE

In a large, heavy-bottomed stockpot, sauté the bacon over medium heat until it softens and some of the fat has rendered out. Add the onion, carrot, and celery and cook until translucent, about 5 minutes. Add the split peas, water, stock, and bay leaf and bring to a boil. Decrease the heat to medium-low and simmer, partially covered, for 1 hour, until the peas are soft.

Remove the bay leaf. Add the lemon zest, lemon juice, and salt and pepper to taste. For a creamier consistency, purée half the soup with an immersion blender or transfer half to a blender and purée.

YIELD: 8 SERVINGS

CHEF'S TIP *If you don't have or don't want to use bacon, but still want the smoky flavor it imparts, you can substitute 1/2 teaspoon liquid smoke instead.*

Cuban Black Bean Soup with Avocado Crema

Black bean soup is one of my favorite wintertime meals because it's warm, filling, and comforting. Don't skip the avocado crema! It is made with only three ingredients, but the zesty avocado and citrus combination takes this soup to the next level of deliciousness.

FOR SOUP:

4	SLICES BACON, DICED
½	POUND (225 G) PORK BUTT OR LOIN, DICED INTO ½-INCH (1.3-CM) CUBES
1	TEASPOON GROUND CUMIN
1	TEASPOON DRIED OREGANO
1	BAY LEAF
5	CLOVES GARLIC, MINCED
½	MEDIUM WHITE ONION, DICED
1	GREEN BELL PEPPER, STEMMED, SEEDED, AND DICED
4	CUPS (940 ML) WATER
4	CUPS (940 ML) CHICKEN STOCK
2	CUPS (500 G) DRIED BLACK BEANS, PICKED THROUGH AND RINSED
	SALT AND PEPPER TO TASTE
1	TABLESPOON (15 ML) LIME JUICE

FOR AVOCADO CREMA:

½	MEDIUM AVOCADO
¼	CUP (60 ML) MEXICAN CREMA OR SOUR CREAM
1	TEASPOON LIME ZEST
	SALT AND PEPPER TO TASTE

OPTIONAL EXTRAS:

8	LIME WEDGES, FOR GARNISH
8	CORN TORTILLAS, WARMED, FOR SERVING

To make the soup: Heat a large, heavy-bottomed stockpot over medium-high heat. Sauté the bacon and pork until golden brown and the bacon fat is rendered.

Decrease the heat to medium-low, then add the cumin, oregano, bay leaf, garlic, onion, and bell pepper and cook until the mixture is fragrant and the onions are soft, about 5 minutes.

Add the water, chicken stock, and black beans to the pot. Cook, covered, over medium-high heat until the soup begins to gently boil. Decrease the heat to a simmer and cook for 2½ to 3 hours, until the beans are tender.

Discard the bay leaf. Transfer about half of the soup to a blender (or use an immersion blender) and blend on high speed, until smooth and creamy. Add the puréed soup back to the pot. Season to taste with salt and pepper and add the lime juice.

To make the avocado crema: Place the avocado, sour cream, lime zest, and a pinch of salt and pepper to a mini food processor. Process for 20 to 30 seconds, or until smooth and creamy.

Serve the soup with a dollop of the crema and a wedge of lime. Warm corn tortillas make this a complete, hearty meal.

YIELD: 8 SERVINGS

CHEF'S TIP *Proper flavor balance will set your cooking apart. Seasoning with salt and pepper is key, but don't forget about acidity, too. A squeeze of lime in this dish brightens the rich soup and makes the flavors pop.*

Creamy Chicken and Rice Soup

Chicken soup is the ultimate comfort food. Making this soup creamy by puréeing some of the rice and adding a bit of cream makes it over the top. For added freshness, stir in frozen peas and chopped parsley at the very end.

8   CUPS (1880 ML) CHICKEN STOCK

2   POUNDS (910 G) BONE-IN CHICKEN BREAST

6   STEMS THYME

2   BAY LEAVES

2   MEDIUM CARROTS, PEELED AND CUT INTO 3 PIECES EACH

2   STALKS CELERY, CUT INTO 3 PIECES EACH

1   ONION, CUT INTO LARGE CHUNKS

4   CLOVES GARLIC, MINCED

1½ CUPS (278 G) LONG-GRAIN WHITE RICE

½   CUP (120 ML) CREAM

    SALT AND PEPPER TO TASTE

In a large, heavy-bottomed stockpot, combine the chicken stock, chicken breast, thyme, bay leaves, carrots, celery, onion, and garlic. Bring to a gentle boil over medium heat, then cover, decrease the heat to low, and simmer for 2 hours, or until the chicken is very tender.

Add the rice and cook until tender, 20 to 25 minutes. Remove the chicken, thyme, bay leaves, carrots, celery, onion, and 2½ cups (412 g) of the rice. Add the cream to the pot, then blend the soup in the pot with an immersion blender, or transfer to a blender and blend until smooth. Place the puréed soup back into the pot.

Discard the bay leaves and thyme. Shred the chicken and dice the carrots, celery, and onion into bite-size pieces. Add everything, including the remaining rice, back into the pot with the puréed soup. Season with salt and pepper to taste.

YIELD: 12 SERVINGS

CHEF'S TIP *Be sure to use bone-in chicken breast if you can. The bone adds incredible flavor to the soup.*

Butternut Squash Soup with Chipotle and Brown Sugar

A hint of smoky, spicy chipotle chile makes a classic velvety butternut squash soup new again.

2   CUPS (470 ML) WATER

4   CUPS (940 ML) CHICKEN OR VEGETABLE
    STOCK

2   POUNDS (910 G) BUTTERNUT SQUASH,
    PEELED AND CUT INTO CHUNKS

1   CUP (160 G) DICED WHITE ONION

½   CUP (65 G) DICED CARROT

½   CUP (50 G) DICED CELERY

1   CHIPOTLE CHILE IN ADOBO SAUCE
    (CANNED), ROUGHLY CHOPPED,
    PLUS 1 TABLESPOON (15 ML) OF THE
    ADOBO SAUCE

1   BAY LEAF

½   CUP (120 ML) HEAVY CREAM

¼   CUP (60 G) LIGHTLY PACKED BROWN
    SUGAR

    SALT AND PEPPER TO TASTE

Place the water, chicken stock, butternut squash, onion, carrot, celery, chipotle chile, adobo sauce, and bay leaf into a large, heavy-bottomed pot. Cover the pot and place over medium heat. Bring to a gentle boil, then decrease the heat to low and simmer for about 1 hour, or until the butternut squash and other vegetables are very soft. Remove the pot from the heat. Remove and discard the bay leaf. Add the cream and brown sugar.

Ladle the soup into a blender and blend until smooth and creamy (this may take a few batches) or use an immersion blender directly in the pot to blend the soup. Season to taste with salt and pepper. Serve hot.

YIELD: 8 SERVINGS

CHEF'S TIP *Use caution when blending hot liquids in a blender! Steam can cause the lid to pop off and hot soup to burst out when you turn it on, so be sure to let the soup cool slightly before blending, put the lid on, and cover with a dish towel, then begin on a low setting and increase the speed gradually.*

Hearty Spiced Red Lentil Soup

The warm spice of ginger and cardamom give this dish an Indian flare. Red lentils really break down when they cook, making this soup thick and creamy without using a blender.

1½ CUPS (330 G) RED LENTILS

4 CUPS (940 ML) CHICKEN STOCK

1 CAN (13.5 OUNCES, OR 400 ML) COCONUT MILK

5 GREEN CARDAMOM PODS, CRUSHED SLIGHTLY WITH YOUR FINGERS

2 STAR ANISE PODS

1 CUP (160 G) DICED WHITE ONION

1 CUP (130 G) DICED CARROT

2 TABLESPOONS (16 G) GRATED GINGER

½ TEASPOON RED PEPPER FLAKES

2 TABLESPOONS (30 ML) LEMON JUICE

SALT AND PEPPER TO TASTE

Rinse the lentils under cold running water until the water runs clear, about 1 minute. Pick out any little stones and discard.

In a large, heavy-bottomed stockpot or Dutch oven, combine the lentils, chicken stock, coconut milk, cardamom pods, star anise pods, onion, carrot, ginger, and red pepper flakes. Bring to a simmer, cover, and cook over low heat for 1 hour, or until the lentils are tender and begin to fall apart.

Remove the cardamom and anise pods, add the lemon juice and salt and pepper to taste, and serve.

✎ YIELD: 6 SERVINGS

✕ CHEF'S TIP *I make a double batch of this soup and freeze half for wintertime lunches on days when I need something quick and easy.*

Roasted Garlic and Tomato Soup

Surprisingly, many canned or restaurant tomato soups are thickened with wheat flour.
This recipe needs no thickener and is full of heavenly mellow roasted garlic and tangy tomato flavor
married by a touch of sweet cream.

2   MEDIUM BULBS GARLIC

1   TEASPOON OLIVE OIL

4   CUPS (940 ML) CHICKEN OR VEGETABLE STOCK

1   CAN (28 OUNCES, OR 790 G) WHOLE PEELED TOMATOES

½   CUP (65 G) CHOPPED CARROT

½   CUP (50 G) CHOPPED CELERY

1   CUP (160 G) CHOPPED WHITE ONION

1   BAY LEAF

½   CUP (120 ML) HEAVY CREAM

SALT AND PEPPER TO TASTE

CHEF'S TIP *For an especially silky consistency, pour the soup through a fine-mesh strainer after you blend it.*

Preheat the oven to 400°F (200°C, or gas mark 6).

Slice off the very tops of the bulbs of garlic to remove some of the papery exterior and expose the garlic cloves. Place the bulbs on a piece of aluminum foil and sprinkle them with the olive oil. Wrap up the bulbs loosely in the foil and bake for 45 minutes, or until soft and tender. Let the bulbs cool until they are easy to handle.

While the garlic bulbs are roasting, prepare the soup. Place the stock, tomatoes, carrot, celery, onion, and bay leaf into a heavy-bottomed stockpot. Place over high heat, bring to a boil, decrease the heat to medium-low, and simmer for about 40 minutes, or until the onion is very tender and translucent. Remove the bay leaf.

Gently separate and peel the papery exterior from each clove of garlic from the bulb and throw them into the pot with the soup. Add the cream, and stir to combine. Ladle the soup into a blender and purée until very smooth (this may take several batches) or use an immersion blender. Season to taste with salt and pepper and serve. This soup also freezes well in an airtight container.

YIELD: 8 SERVINGS

VARIATION *This gorgeous soup can easily be made dairy-free using soy or coconut milk in place of the cream, or omit it altogether for a tangier alternative.*

Italian White Bean Soup

In this recipe I use dried beans, which take longer to cook but result in a thicker, richer broth as the beans release their starch.

4	CLOVES GARLIC, CHOPPED
½	FENNEL BULB, DICED
2	CARROTS, PEELED AND DICED
1	STALK CELERY, DICED
1	ONION, DICED
1	CUP (250 G) DRIED CANNELLINI BEANS, PICKED THROUGH AND RINSED
2	STEMS ROSEMARY
4	STEMS THYME
1	CUP (100 G) GRATED PARMESAN CHEESE, PLUS THE RIND
6	CUPS (1410 ML) CHICKEN OR VEGETABLE STOCK
4	CUPS (940 ML) WATER
1	BUNCH ESCAROLE (ABOUT 1 POUND [455 G]), TOUGH STEMS REMOVED, ROUGHLY CHOPPED
	SALT AND PEPPER TO TASTE

Place the garlic, fennel, carrots, celery, onion, cannellini beans, rosemary, thyme, Parmesan rind, stock, and water into a large pot. Cover the pot and slowly bring to a slight boil over medium heat. Set the lid of the pot askew, decrease the heat to a simmer, and cook for 3 hours, or until the beans are very tender.

Remove the Parmesan rind, rosemary, and thyme from the pot and discard. Add the chopped escarole and cook for another 10 minutes, or until the escarole is tender. Season to taste with salt and pepper, ladle into bowls, and garnish with the Parmesan cheese.

YIELD: 8 SERVINGS

✗ CHEF'S TIP *The outer rind of Parmesan cheese is very hard, so it is typically discarded, but I save mine in a zipper-top bag in the freezer because they are great for adding flavor to soups such as this one.*

Steak Chili with Pickled Jalapeños and Butternut Squash

This chili is an all-around crowd-pleaser. It is super spicy and has a touch of sweetness from the butternut squash. This is a perfect make-ahead dish for a busy week or game-night entertaining.

2 POUNDS (910 G) BOTTOM ROUND OF BEEF, CUT INTO BITE-SIZE CUBES

SALT AND PEPPER TO TASTE

1 TABLESPOON (15 ML) CANOLA OIL

2 CUPS (320 G) DICED WHITE ONION

6 CLOVES GARLIC, MINCED

½ CUP (65 G) PICKLED JALAPEÑOS

2 BAY LEAVES

1 CUP (250 G) DRIED BLACK BEANS, PICKED THROUGH AND RINSED

3 CUPS (705 ML) BEEF STOCK

1 CAN (14.5 OUNCES, OR 410 G) CRUSHED TOMATOES

2 TABLESPOONS (40 G) MOLASSES

¼ CUP (35 G) CORNMEAL

1 TABLESPOON (7.5 G) CHILI POWDER

2 TEASPOONS GARLIC POWDER

1 TEASPOON GROUND CUMIN

1 TEASPOON GROUND CORIANDER

1 TEASPOON GROUND CINNAMON

1 POUND (455 G) BUTTERNUT SQUASH, PEELED AND CUT INTO BITE-SIZE CUBES

Preheat the oven to 300°F (150°C, or gas mark 2).

Heat a large, oven-proof, heavy-bottomed stockpot over high heat. Season the bottom round with salt and pepper. Add the canola oil to the hot pan, then add the cubed beef. Cook for 7 to 8 minutes, stirring once, until the meat is browned.

Add the onion, garlic, pickled jalapeños, bay leaves, black beans, beef stock, tomatoes, molasses, cornmeal, chili powder, garlic powder, cumin, coriander, and cinnamon to the pot. Bring to a gentle boil, then cover and place the pot in the oven for 2½ hours.

Add the butternut squash and cook for another hour, or until the beans are cooked and the butternut squash is tender. Remove the bay leaves. Season with salt and pepper to taste.

YIELD: 6 SERVINGS

CHEF'S TIP *I use leftovers of this chili to make the ultimate nachos! Place tortilla chips on a baking sheet, top them with shredded cheese, and place in the oven to melt. Top with the warm steak chili, sour cream, and diced tomatoes. Dig in!*

VARIATION *To make in a slow cooker: Sear the bottom round as described above. Transfer to a 4- to 6-quart (3.6- to 5.4-L) slow cooker and add the onion, garlic, pickled jalapeños, bay leaves, black beans, beef stock, tomatoes, molasses, cornmeal, chili powder, garlic powder, cumin, coriander, and cinnamon. Cover and cook on high for 5 to 6 hours or on low for 7 to 8 hours. During the last 2 hours of cooking, add the butternut squash. Remove the bay leaves before serving. Season with salt and pepper to taste.*

Chapter

7

ENTRÉES *for* EVERYONE

Crispy Pancetta and Pea Risotto

Despite its reputation, this classic Italian course is not difficult to make and has the wow factor of a "fancy" dish. In this recipe, the salty pancetta is balanced by the sweet fresh peas, making it impossible to resist. Risotto is always best served right away.

6 OUNCES (170 G) PANCETTA, THINLY SLICED

3 CUPS (705 ML) CHICKEN STOCK

1 TABLESPOON (14 G) UNSALTED BUTTER

1 ONION, DICED

1 CUP (195 G) ARBORIO OR CARNAROLI RICE

1 CUP (235 ML) DRY WHITE WINE

1 CUP (130 G) FROZEN OR BLANCHED, FRESH PEAS

⅓ CUP (35 G) PARMESAN CHEESE, PLUS MORE FOR GARNISH, IF DESIRED

SALT AND PEPPER TO TASTE

CHEF'S TIP *Risotto should be thin enough to "flow" into a soft puddle when spooned into a dish, never gummy or thick. Just add a little more chicken stock to adjust the consistency if it thickens up on you.*

Preheat the oven to 350°F (180°C, or gas mark 4).

Place the pancetta slices on a baking sheet lined with foil. Bake for 8 to 10 minutes, until crisp. Let cool, then reserve 4 whole slices of the pancetta for garnish later. Crumble the remaining pancetta into a small bowl and set aside.

In a medium saucepan, heat the chicken stock to a simmer, cover, and keep warm on low heat.

In a large skillet over medium heat, melt the butter. Add the onion and sauté until translucent, about 5 minutes. Add the rice and stir until the rice is fully coated with butter. Add the wine and cook, stirring occasionally, until the wine is absorbed into the rice.

Add about 1 cup (235 ml) of the stock and stir until the stock is absorbed. Repeat this process two more times until all the stock is incorporated and the rice is tender, making sure that between each addition the stock is mostly absorbed before adding more. This process will take about 20 minutes, and the rice should be tender but not mushy.

Take the rice off of the heat and stir in the peas, Parmesan cheese, and crumbled pancetta. Season with salt and pepper to taste. Divide among 4 plates, then garnish with the remaining slices of whole, crispy pancetta and extra Parmesan cheese, if desired.

YIELD: 4 SERVINGS

New York Strip Steaks with Red Wine Sauce

In Ruth Reichl's book Garlic and Sapphires *she talks about her father's advice for seasoning steak:*
"The secret to a great steak is that when you think you have enough salt, you add some more."
A little red wine butter sauce doesn't hurt, either. This steak is perfection, and really easy, too!

4   NEW YORK STRIP STEAKS (8 TO 10
    OUNCES, OR 225 TO 280 G EACH)

    SALT AND PEPPER TO TASTE

1   TABLESPOON (15 ML) CANOLA OIL

2   TABLESPOONS (20 G) MINCED SHALLOT
    (ABOUT 1 SHALLOT)

1½ CUPS (355 ML) DRY RED WINE

4   TABLESPOONS (56 G) COLD UNSALTED
    BUTTER, CUT INTO CHUNKS

1   TABLESPOON (2.5 G) MINCED CHERVIL OR
    PARSLEY

> ✗ **CHEF'S TIP** *Never use "cooking
> wine" in your recipes. It's often
> loaded with salt. Instead, always
> cook with a wine you would drink,
> and then you can serve the rest
> with the meal. When I'm cooking
> with wine, I almost always have a
> glass in my hand while I work: it's
> good for the soul!*

Season both sides of the steaks generously with salt and pepper.

Heat a large, heavy-bottomed sauté pan over high heat. Add the canola oil, and when the oil just begins to smoke, gently place the steaks into the pan. Cook for 2 to 3 minutes per side for medium-rare, or longer, depending on your desired doneness.

Transfer the steaks to a plate, cover with aluminum foil, and set aside to rest.

Place the sauté pan back on the stove and decrease the heat to medium. Add the shallot and sauté for 1 minute to soften. Add the wine to the pan and increase the heat to high. Cook for 3 to 4 more minutes, or until the wine is reduced by two-thirds and you have about ½ cup (120 ml) of liquid.

Add the butter, a few pieces at a time, whisking as you go to emulsify the sauce and thicken it. When all of the butter is melted and the sauce is thick, season with salt and pepper and add the chervil.

Place a steak on each of 4 plates, then spoon the red wine sauce over them and serve immediately.

▪ **YIELD: 4 SERVINGS**

Double Garlic Roasted Chicken

A garlic lover's dream, this chicken is the ultimate garlic treat. The chicken is smeared with mellow and nutty roasted garlic, while garlicky compound butter under the skin adds another layer of depth. Leftovers make great chicken salad!

1   BULB GARLIC PLUS 6 CLOVES, DIVIDED

1   TEASPOON OLIVE OIL

4   TABLESPOONS (56 G) UNSALTED BUTTER, SOFTENED

2   TEASPOONS FRESHLY GRATED LEMON ZEST

1   TEASPOON SALT, PLUS MORE TO TASTE

2   TABLESPOONS (8 G) ROUGHLY CHOPPED FRESH PARSLEY

1   ROASTING CHICKEN (3 TO 4 POUNDS, OR 1365 TO 1820 G)

½   ONION, ROUGHLY CHOPPED

1   STALK CELERY, ROUGHLY CHOPPED

1   CARROT, ROUGHLY CHOPPED

    PEPPER TO TASTE

CHEF'S TIP *The secret to roasted chicken with a crispy skin is high heat. If you find that the chicken starts to become too brown, don't cover it. Covering the chicken with foil can make the skin soggy by trapping steam. Instead, just lower the oven temperature about 25°F (12°C).*

Preheat the oven to 350°F (180°C, or gas mark 4).

Cut the top ¼ inch (6 mm) off the head of garlic so that the tops of the cloves are exposed. Drizzle with the olive oil and wrap tightly in aluminum foil. Roast the garlic bulb for about 45 minutes, or until the garlic is tender. Let cool slightly, then squeeze each clove out of the skin, mash, and set aside.

Increase the oven temperature to 425°F (220°C, or gas mark 7). Mince the remaining 6 cloves garlic. Make the compound butter by mixing together the minced garlic, butter, lemon zest, salt, and parsley. Set aside.

Place the chicken in the roasting pan. Put the onion, celery, and carrot inside the cavity of the chicken. Fold the wing tips of the chicken underneath the bird (they should stay in place on their own). Working carefully, use your fingers to separate the skin of the chicken from the meat. Take a little bit of compound butter at a time, and rub directly onto the chicken, under the skin. Smear the mashed roasted garlic all over the top of the chicken, this time right onto the skin. Season generously with salt and pepper.

Roast for about 1 hour and 15 minutes, or until the juices run clear when you cut into the thigh. Allow the chicken to sit for 20 minutes before carving.

YIELD: 4 SERVINGS

Seafood Paella

Paella is a traditional Spanish dish from Valencia. Bomba rice is the traditional rice variety used, but it is hard to find and can be expensive. Here, I call for Arborio rice, which is a good substitute and is found in most grocery stores. Use the largest sea scallops you can find, preferably size U-10 if it's labeled.

2	TABLESPOONS (30 ML) OLIVE OIL
2	DRIED SPANISH CHORIZO SAUSAGES, CUT INTO CHUNKS
1	ONION, DICED
4	CLOVES GARLIC, MINCED
2	CUPS (390 G) ARBORIO RICE
3	CUPS (705 ML) CHICKEN STOCK
1	PINCH OF SAFFRON THREADS
1	CAN (14 OUNCES, OR 392 G) DICED TOMATOES
2	ROASTED RED PEPPERS, STORE-BOUGHT OR HOMEMADE (SEE PAGE 106), SLICED
½	CUP (65 G) FRESH OR FROZEN GREEN PEAS
12	PEELED, DEVEINED SHRIMP
6	LARGE SEA SCALLOPS, CUT IN HALF INTO THIN ROUNDS
12	LITTLENECK CLAMS
4	SQUID TUBES, CLEANED AND SLICED INTO RINGS
	SALT AND PEPPER TO TASTE
1	LEMON, CUT INTO 6 WEDGES

Preheat the oven to 350°F (180°C, or gas mark 4).

In a large oven-proof sauté pan or cast-iron skillet, heat the olive oil over medium-high heat. Add the chorizo and sauté for 2 to 3 minutes, until the fat begins to render out of the sausage. Add the onion and garlic and cook until soft, about 5 minutes. Add the rice and sauté for 2 minutes, stirring to coat each grain with olive oil. Add the chicken stock, saffron, and canned diced tomatoes and their juice, cover with foil, and cook over medium-low heat for 20 minutes, or until the rice is almost tender.

Uncover the pan, add the sliced red peppers and peas, increase the heat to high, and cook to brown the bottom of the rice and make a crust, about 5 minutes. Lift a bit of the rice with a spoon or spatula to check whether the crust has formed and is brown without burning. This is called the socarrat and is essential to the perfect paella.

Season the shrimp, scallops, clams, and squid with salt and pepper. Arrange on top of the paella, cover with foil, and bake for 10 to 15 minutes, or until the clams have opened and the shrimp are cooked through. Remove the foil, discard any clams that haven't opened, and garnish with the lemon wedges. Serve this directly out of the pan with a large serving spoon.

YIELD: 6 SERVINGS

CHEF'S TIP *A traditional paella pan is made out of carbon steel or stainless steel with a round, flat bottom and shallow sides with two handles. If you have one, you will be able to skip the step of turning up the heat to form the socarrat because these thin pans are made to give this dish its signature crust.*

Red Snapper en Papillote

Baking fish in parchment (en papillote) is one of my favorite ways to cook it.
It allows you to cook with no oil at all and produces tender, moist, and flavorful results.

4   BONELESS, SKINLESS FILLETS OF RED SNAPPER (ABOUT 5 OUNCES, OR 140 G EACH)

½   CUP (75 G) JULIENNED BELL PEPPER

½   CUP (38 G) JULIENNED SNOW PEAS

½   CUP (50 G) THINLY SLICED ASPARAGUS

1   SMALL TOMATO, DICED

¼   CUP (60 ML) FRESHLY SQUEEZED ORANGE JUICE

2   TEASPOONS ORANGE ZEST

    SALT AND PEPPER TO TASTE

+ VARIATION *Any quick-cooking vegetable can be used for these. I like baby spinach and zucchini as well.*

Preheat the oven to 375°F (190°C, or gas mark 5).

Cut four 12-inch (30-cm) squares of parchment paper. Fold each square in half and cut into a teardrop shape (when you open it up it should look like a heart).

Place the hearts of parchment sideways on a flat surface. Place 1 fillet of snapper on the bottom half of each piece of parchment paper, snug up against the seam where the paper was folded. Top each fillet with an equal amount of julienned bell pepper, snow peas, sliced asparagus, and diced tomato.

Sprinkle each fillet with about 1 tablespoon (15 ml) orange juice and ½ teaspoon orange zest. Season to taste with salt and pepper. Fold the parchment over the top of the fish, then start at one end and make folds along the edge of the parchment paper to seal the fish into little packages.

Place the packages on a large baking sheet and bake for about 17 minutes, or until the packages puff, indicating they are full of hot steam.

Remove from the oven, cut a slit into the top of the parchment along the folded seam, then roll back the parchment to display the steamed fish and vegetables. Use a spatula to transfer each package to a plate and serve directly in the paper.

YIELD: 4 SERVINGS

Thai Chicken Peanut Curry

Often called rama curry, this spicy peanut sauce gets its kick from fragrant red curry paste. Because the sauce is so rich and flavorful, I serve this very simply over quinoa or brown rice with lots of steamed broccoli.

2½ POUNDS (1138 G) BONELESS, SKINLESS CHICKEN THIGHS, CUT INTO 1-INCH (2.5-CM) PIECES

2 TABLESPOONS (16 G) CORNSTARCH

1 TEASPOON CANOLA OIL

1 CUP (235 ML) CHICKEN STOCK OR WATER

3 TABLESPOONS (48 G) THAI RED CURRY PASTE

½ CUP (130 G) ALL-NATURAL CREAMY PEANUT BUTTER

2 TABLESPOONS (30 ML) FISH SAUCE

2 TABLESPOONS (30 G) BROWN SUGAR

3 CLOVES GARLIC, MINCED

1 TABLESPOON (8 G) GRATED FRESH GINGER

Heat a large sauté pan over high heat. Coat the chicken pieces in cornstarch, then add the canola oil and the chicken to the pan. Cook for 12 to 15 minutes, stirring only once or twice, until the chicken is cooked through and is golden brown.

While the chicken cooks, whisk together the chicken stock, red curry paste, peanut butter, fish sauce, and brown sugar in a small bowl. Set aside.

When the chicken is golden brown, drain off any excess fat from the pan by pouring the chicken into a strainer and letting any drippings drain out. Place the chicken back into the pan, add the garlic and ginger, and cook for 1 to 2 minutes to soften the garlic and release the flavors.

Add the red curry mixture to the pan and decrease the heat to low. Simmer for 2 to 3 more minutes to heat the sauce through and combine the flavors. Serve immediately.

YIELD: 6 SERVINGS

CHEF'S TIP *Fish sauce is very salty, so there is no need for additional salt in this recipe. You can adjust the spiciness of the dish with more or less curry paste, depending on your tastes.*

Asparagus and Leek Tart with Polenta Crust

Traditionally, polenta was a rustic Italian peasant's dish. In recent years it has grown in popularity and can be found on the menus of many gourmet restaurants. Here, it makes the perfect gluten-free crust for this quiche-like tart.

FOR THE CRUST:

2 CUPS (470 ML) CHICKEN STOCK

½ CUP (70 G) YELLOW CORNMEAL (POLENTA), MEDIUM GRIND

   SALT AND PEPPER TO TASTE

FOR THE FILLING:

1 TABLESPOON (15 ML) OLIVE OIL

2 LEEKS, WHITE PARTS ONLY, THINLY SLICED AND WELL RINSED

1 TABLESPOON (15 ML) MARSALA WINE

1¼ CUPS (295 ML) MILK

2 EGGS

¼ TEASPOON SALT

½ CUP (60 G) SHREDDED GRUYÈRE CHEESE

1 BUNCH ASPARAGUS, TRIMMED TO 4 INCHES (10 CM) LONG

CHEF'S TIP *Leeks have a tendency to be very sandy. To clean, slice them, place in a large bowl of cold water, separate the layers of the leeks with your fingers, then let sit for a few minutes. Any sand and sediment in the leeks will fall to the bottom of the bowl. Lift the leeks out of the bowl with your hands and onto a paper towel to drain, then repeat the process once more.*

Preheat the oven to 400°F (200°C, or gas mark 6).

To make the crust: In a medium saucepan, bring the chicken stock to a boil over high heat. Whisk in the polenta, decrease the heat to low, and cook for about 15 minutes, stirring constantly, until the polenta is thick and no longer feels gritty. Season with salt and pepper to taste.

Pour the polenta into a 9-inch (23-cm) tart pan or pie plate and let sit for 2 minutes to cool slightly. Cover with plastic wrap and press down on the plastic wrap to flatten the polenta on the bottom and up the sides of the pan. Let cool to room temperature until firm.

Remove the plastic wrap and prick all over with a fork. Bake for 15 minutes, or until golden brown. Set aside to cool.

To make the filling: Decrease the oven to 350°F (180°C, or gas mark 4). In a medium sauté pan, heat the olive oil over medium heat, then add the leeks. Sauté until softened, about 5 minutes, then set aside.

In a medium bowl, whisk together the Marsala, milk, eggs, and salt. Stir in the Gruyère and leeks, and pour into the crust. Arrange the spears of asparagus on top, pointing outward in a circular shape. Bake for 20 minutes, or until the middle of the tart is just set. Allow to cool to room temperature before cutting.

YIELD: 6 SERVINGS

Shrimp Biryani
(Shrimp and Rice Pilaf with Indian Spices)

Fragrant basmati rice is the key to this heady dish, chock-full of exotic Indian spices.

2 CUPS (380 G) BASMATI RICE

PINCH OF SAFFRON THREADS

SALT AND PEPPER TO TASTE

1 CUP (235 ML) COCONUT MILK

2 CUPS (470 ML) WATER

2 TABLESPOONS (28 G) UNSALTED BUTTER

1 ONION, DICED

4 CLOVES GARLIC, MINCED

1 TABLESPOON (8 G) GRATED FRESH
GINGER

1 SPICY GREEN CHILE (SUCH AS SERRANO
OR THAI BIRD), MINCED

2 CUPS (360 G) DICED FRESH TOMATOES
(ABOUT 2 TOMATOES)

½ TEASPOON BLACK PEPPERCORNS

1 TEASPOON GARAM MASALA

¼ TEASPOON TURMERIC

3 CARDAMOM PODS, CRUSHED OPEN WITH
YOUR PALM

PINCH OF CAYENNE PEPPER

2 TABLESPOONS (30 ML) FRESHLY
SQUEEZED LEMON JUICE

2 TABLESPOONS (2 G) CHOPPED CILANTRO

1 POUND (455 G) PEELED, DEVEINED
SHRIMP

Rinse the rice in a fine-mesh strainer under running water until the water runs clear. Place the rice into a saucepan with the saffron, a pinch of salt and pepper, the coconut milk, and the water. Bring to a boil, cover, decrease the heat to low, and cook for about 10 minutes.

While the rice is coming to a boil, melt the butter in a heavy-bottomed pot or Dutch oven with a tight-fitting lid. Add the onion, garlic, ginger, and green chile and sauté over medium heat until the onion becomes translucent, about 5 minutes. Add the diced tomatoes, black peppercorns, garam masala, turmeric, cardamom, and cayenne pepper. Season with salt and pepper and cook over medium heat for 7 minutes, or until the tomatoes have softened and released their juices, and the mixture thickens slightly. Add the lemon juice and chopped cilantro and stir to combine.

Season the shrimp with salt and pepper and arrange on top of the tomato mixture. Pour the rice and the coconut milk mixture that has been cooking for 10 minutes on top of the shrimp; you should have three layers—do not combine them yet! Cover tightly and cook for an additional 8 to 10 minutes, or until the rice is cooked through.

Remove from the heat and let sit, covered, for 5 minutes. Stir to combine the rice, shrimp, and tomato mixture, and serve.

 YIELD: 5 SERVINGS

CHEF'S TIP *Garam masala is an Indian spice blend you can find in most stores. Substitute curry powder if you can't find it, but leave out the turmeric because most curry blends contain it.*

Grilled Lamb Kebabs with Creamy Tzatziki Sauce

I love this easy marinade for lamb. It is made with a whole lemon, so you get all of those intricate flavors in the dish: the tang of the lemon juice, the fragrant peel, and the bitter pith. Those complex flavors all work together with garlic and oregano for authentic Greek flavor. I serve these lamb skewers with a simple salad of romaine lettuce, tomatoes, and kalamata olives.

FOR LAMB KEBABS:

1   WHOLE LEMON, ROUGHLY CHOPPED

4   CLOVES GARLIC

2   TABLESPOONS (30 ML) OLIVE OIL

4   STEMS FRESH OREGANO OR
    1 TABLESPOON (3 G) DRIED

2   TEASPOONS SALT

2   POUNDS (910 G) TRIMMED BONELESS
    LEG OF LAMB, CUT INTO 1-INCH (2.5-CM)
    CUBES

FOR TZATZIKI SAUCE:

1   CUP (230 G) PLAIN GREEK YOGURT,
    STORE-BOUGHT OR HOMEMADE (PAGE 77),

½   CUP (60 G) GRATED CUCUMBER

1   TABLESPOON (15 ML) FRESH LEMON
    JUICE

1   CLOVE GARLIC, GRATED

    SALT AND PEPPER TO TASTE

Soak 12 wooden skewers in water (or if using metal skewers, skip this step).

Place the lemon, garlic, olive oil, oregano, and salt into the bowl of a food processor or mini chopper. Pulse until all of the ingredients are combined and roughly chopped, about 4 or 5 pulses. Add the mixture to a gallon-size zipper-top bag along with the lamb cubes and marinate in the refrigerator for at least 1 hour or up to 6 hours.

To make the tzatziki sauce: Place the yogurt in a small bowl. Squeeze out any excess liquid from the grated cucumber by gently squeezing it in the palm of your hand over the sink. Add the cucumber, lemon juice, and garlic to the bowl with the yogurt. Season to taste with salt and pepper and stir to combine. Refrigerate until ready to use.

When the lamb is marinated, wipe off any excess marinade from the pieces of lamb, and thread the meat onto the 12 skewers. Preheat a grill or grill pan to high, then grill the skewers for 6 to 8 minutes, turning occasionally, until charred and brown on the outside, but still pink on the inside. Serve hot with the tzatziki sauce on the side.

❚ YIELD: 4 SERVINGS

✚ VARIATION *This recipe is delicious with chicken, too!*

Perfect Pulled Pork

It's magic to watch this dish come together. After slowly simmering for 6 hours, the pork will literally fall to pieces. The sauce is not too sweet, and not too vinegary. I love it served with potato salad and coleslaw, but it would also make delicious tacos tucked into soft, warm corn tortillas.

1   CUP (235 ML) CHICKEN STOCK

1   CUP (240 G) KETCHUP

¼   CUP (60 ML) APPLE CIDER VINEGAR

2   TABLESPOONS (40 G) MOLASSES

¼   CUP (60 G) LIGHTLY PACKED BROWN
    SUGAR

3   CLOVES GARLIC, CHOPPED

1   ONION, FINELY CHOPPED

1   CHIPOTLE CHILE PEPPER IN ADOBO
    SAUCE, FINELY MINCED, PLUS
    1 TABLESPOON (15 ML) ADOBO SAUCE

2   TEASPOONS ONION POWDER

2   TEASPOONS GARLIC POWDER

3   POUNDS (1360 G) BONELESS PORK BUTT

Preheat the oven to 325°F (170°C, or gas mark 3).

Combine all of the ingredients in a large Dutch oven or heavy-bottomed stockpot. Cover with a lid, and bring to a boil over medium-high heat.

Transfer the covered pot to the oven. Cook for 3 hours, then turn the meat over, and cook for 3 more hours, or until the meat begins to easily break apart when pierced with a fork.

Transfer the pork to a plate and set aside. Place the pot with the cooking liquid over high heat and bring to a boil. Cook for 10 to 15 minutes, or until the sauce is thickened and reduced by half. Use a ladle to skim off any excess fat from the top of the sauce, and discard.

Meanwhile, using 2 forks, pull and shred the pork into bite-size pieces. Discard any large pieces of fat. Add the pulled pork back into the pot with the sauce. Stir to combine, then serve.

YIELD: 8 SERVINGS

CHEF'S TIP *This recipe can also be made in a slow cooker set on high for the same amount of time. Just transfer the cooking liquid to a saucepan to reduce it after cooking.*

Vegetable Sushi Rolls with Spicy Sauce

This veggie sushi makes the perfect lunch, appetizer, or light dinner. Chop the vegetables while the rice cooks, then make the spicy sauce while it cools, and this dish will come together in no time!

FOR SUSHI RICE:

2   CUPS (390 G) SUSHI RICE

2   CUPS (470 ML) WATER

3   TABLESPOONS (45 ML) RICE VINEGAR

3   TABLESPOONS (38 G) SUGAR

2   TEASPOONS SALT

FOR SPICY SAUCE:

⅔   CUP (150 G) MAYONNAISE

1   CLOVE GARLIC, MINCED

3   TABLESPOONS (45 ML) SRIRACHA SAUCE

FOR ROLLS:

8   SHEETS ROASTED NORI

1   CUP (120 G) JULIENNED CUCUMBER

1   CUP (150 G) JULIENNED RED BELL PEP-PER

½   CUP (55 G) GRATED CARROT

1   AVOCADO, PEELED, PITTED, AND THINLY SLICED

8   ASPARAGUS SPEARS, STEAMED

PREPARED WASABI, FOR SERVING

PICKLED GINGER, FOR SERVING

> ✕ **CHEF'S TIP** *A sushi rolling mat is the easiest way to roll sushi. If you don't have one, a piece of waxed paper or heavy-duty aluminum foil can be substituted in a pinch.*

To make the sushi rice: Rinse the rice in a fine-mesh strainer until the water runs clear. Let the rice sit in the strainer for about 30 minutes to dry (when the grains of rice crack, they are ready to cook).

Place the rice into a saucepan with the water and bring to a boil. Cover and cook for 15 minutes. Remove from the heat and leave covered for 5 more minutes.

Place the rice into a nonmetallic baking dish or bowl. Add the vinegar, sugar, and salt and stir with a silicone spatula to combine. Let cool to room temperature.

Meanwhile, to make the spicy sauce: Combine the mayonnaise, garlic, and sriracha sauce in a small bowl. Set aside.

Fill a small bowl with cold water and place it near you. Assemble the sushi by placing 1 sheet of nori (shiny side down) onto a sushi rolling mat. Dip your fingers into the bowl of water, then scoop about ½ cup (82 g) of rice onto the bottom half of the nori with your fingers. Use your fingers to gently and evenly distribute the rice to completely cover the bottom half of the nori with a thin layer. Take care not to mash or compress the rice too much.

Place a few pieces of each veggie and 1 asparagus spear lengthwise across the center of the rice on the nori. Use your finger dipped in water to moisten the top ½ inch (1.3 cm) of the nori (this will help the roll seal after you roll it).

Use the sushi mat to roll the sushi from the bottom (the rice end) up and then away from you. Keep pushing the sushi mat away from you to completely roll the sushi. Place the roll seam side down on a cutting board. Repeat to make the remaining 7 rolls.

Cut each roll in half, and then cut each half into thirds, so that each roll is cut into 6 even pieces. Arrange the pieces on a platter with the wasabi and pickled ginger to garnish. Drizzle the rolls with the spicy sauce and serve.

◥ **YIELD: 8 SUSHI ROLLS**

Seared Scallops with Creamy Corn and Spinach Sauce

Scallops always make an impressive meal, and they are much easier to make than most people think. I spoon a small amount of the savory sauce onto each scallop before serving.

16 LARGE SEA SCALLOPS
    SALT AND PEPPER TO TASTE
2   TEASPOONS CANOLA OIL
2   CLOVES GARLIC, MINCED
½   CUP (75 G) CORN KERNELS
½   CUP (120 ML) HALF-AND-HALF (OR ¼ CUP [60 ML] EACH MILK AND HEAVY CREAM)
1   CUP (30 G) BABY SPINACH LEAVES, THINLY SLICED
1   TEASPOON LEMON ZEST

> ✕ **CHEF'S TIP** *When buying scallops, make sure you are buying "dry" scallops rather than "wet packed," which have moisture added and will never brown properly. Ask at the fish counter if you're unsure.*

Remove the small muscle from the side of the scallop by pulling it off with your fingers. (This muscle holds the scallop in its shell and is very tough. You'll recognize it as tab running along the side of the scallop.) Season the scallops with salt and pepper.

Heat a large sauté pan or cast-iron skillet over high heat. When the pan is very hot, add the canola oil. When the oil just begins to smoke, add the scallops. Sear for 2 to 3 minutes without moving the scallops in the pan (this will allow them to get a nice brown crust), then flip and cook for 1 to 2 minutes longer to brown the other side. The scallops should be medium-rare inside. Transfer to a plate and cover loosely with foil to stay warm.

Decrease the heat to medium, add the garlic and the corn kernels, and sauté for 2 to 3 minutes to soften the garlic. Add the half-and-half and increase the heat to high. Cook for 2 to 3 minutes, or until the mixture thickens and reduces slightly. Use an immersion blender or a regular blender to purée until smooth. Add the mixture back into the pan, add the spinach and lemon zest, and cook until the spinach is wilted, about 1 minute. Season to taste with salt and pepper, then spoon over the scallops and serve.

▌ YIELD: 4 SERVINGS

Almond-Crusted Brown Butter Trout

A panfried almond coating gives a crunchy, flavorful exterior to this tender, savory fish.
This impressive dish comes together in no time and looks very elegant. Ask at the fish counter that the
bones and skin be removed from the fish so you can save time.

4   BONELESS, SKINLESS FILLETS OF TROUT
    SALT AND PEPPER TO TASTE

¼   CUP (32 G) CORNSTARCH

1   EGG, BEATEN

1   CUP (120 G) FINELY CHOPPED ALMONDS

5   TABLESPOONS (70 G) UNSALTED BUTTER,
    DIVIDED

2   TABLESPOONS (30 ML) FRESHLY
    SQUEEZED LEMON JUICE

1   TABLESPOON (2 G) CHOPPED FRESH
    CHERVIL OR PARSLEY

CHEF'S TIP *Be careful not to let*
the pan get too hot! The almond
coating and the butter will burn
and become bitter if heated too
aggressively.

Season both sides of the trout with salt and pepper and dust with the cornstarch. Place the beaten egg in a shallow bowl and spread the almonds on a plate. Dip the fillets into the egg and then dredge in the chopped almonds. Press the almonds on to make sure the fillet is fully coated.

In a large sauté pan over medium heat, melt 3 tablespoons (42 g) of the butter. Once the butter is melted and slightly bubbling, add the trout and cook for about 2 minutes per side. The almonds should be golden and crisp. Transfer to a plate and set aside.

Add the remaining 2 tablespoons (28 g) butter to the pan and cook over medium heat until the butter is light brown and nutty smelling. Remove from the heat and add the lemon juice, chervil, and a pinch of salt and pepper. Stir to combine, then spoon a small amount of the sauce over each fillet of trout and serve.

YIELD: 4 SERVINGS

Burgundy Beef Stew

This is a thick, rich, and savory classic French stew just perfect for a winter meal.
You can use any root vegetables you like, though I typically use a combination
of turnips, potatoes, and carrots.

3 TABLESPOONS (45 ML) CANOLA OIL, DIVIDED

2 CUPS (140 G) SLICED MUSHROOMS OF YOUR CHOICE

2½ POUNDS (1138 G) BOTTOM OR TOP ROUND OF BEEF, CUT INTO 1-INCH (2.5-CM) CUBES

2 TEASPOONS SALT

¼ TEASPOON FRESHLY GROUND BLACK PEPPER

¼ CUP (32 G) CORNSTARCH

1 ONION, DICED

6 CLOVES GARLIC, CHOPPED

1 CAN (14.5 OUNCES, OR 406 G) DICED TOMATOES

2 CUPS (470 ML) RED WINE

2 CUPS (470 ML) LOW-SODIUM BEEF STOCK

2 STEMS THYME

2 BAY LEAVES

2 CUPS (220 G) PEELED, CHUNKED ROOT VEGETABLES, SUCH AS POTATOES, CARROTS, PARSNIPS, TURNIPS, AND/OR RUTABAGAS

Heat a large, heavy-bottomed stockpot over high heat. Add 1 tablespoon (15 ml) of the canola oil and the sliced mushrooms and cook for 5 to 6 minutes, or until they release their juices and turn golden brown. Transfer the mushrooms to a plate and set aside.

Season the cubes of beef with the salt and pepper and dust them with the cornstarch. Add 1 tablespoon (15 ml) of the canola oil to the pan. Add half of the beef cubes to the pan and cook for about 10 minutes, or until golden brown. Stir only once or twice to allow the cubes to brown.

Transfer the beef cubes to the plate with the mushrooms and repeat with the remaining 1 tablespoon (15 ml) oil and the remaining beef cubes. Once they are golden brown, add all of the meat and mushrooms back into the pot.

Add the onion, garlic, diced tomatoes, red wine, beef stock, thyme, and bay leaves to the pot. Bring to a low boil, then decrease the heat to low, cover, and simmer for 3 hours, or until the meat is tender. Add the root vegetables and cook for another 30 minutes, uncovered, or until the vegetables are tender and the stew has thickened. Remove the bay leaves and stems of the thyme before serving.

YIELD: 8 SERVINGS

CHEF'S TIP *Notice that thick film the sauce forms along the edge of the pot as the stew cooks down and reduces? It's full of flavor! Use a rubber spatula to scrape the goodness back into your stew on occasion. It will keep all the flavor in the stew and make cleanup easier later!*

Chicken with Sun-Dried Tomato Cream Sauce

With very few ingredients and only one pan, you can make this mouthwatering chicken in a tangy and rich sun-dried tomato cream sauce in about half an hour. Serve with steamed rice and a simple green vegetable for a beautiful dinner.

2   POUNDS (910 G) BONELESS, SKINLESS CHICKEN THIGHS

    SALT AND PEPPER TO TASTE

3   TABLESPOONS (24 G) CORNSTARCH

1   TABLESPOON (15 ML) OLIVE OIL

4   CLOVES GARLIC, MINCED

¼   CUP (60 ML) MARSALA OR WHITE WINE

¼   CUP (60 ML) HEAVY CREAM

½   CUP (120 ML) CHICKEN STOCK

½   CUP (50 G) THINLY SLICED SUN-DRIED TOMATOES (NOT PACKED IN OIL)

Season the chicken well with salt and pepper, then dredge in the cornstarch. Heat a large sauté pan over high heat. Add the olive oil, then the chicken, and cook for 3 to 4 minutes per side, or until golden brown.

Add the garlic to the pan and cook for 1 minute to soften. Add the wine and cook over high heat for about 2 minutes, or until reduced by half. Add the cream, chicken stock, and sun-dried tomatoes.

Bring the mixture to a boil, then decrease the heat to medium-low. Simmer for 20 minutes, or until the chicken is tender and the sauce is thick and creamy.

YIELD: 6 SERVINGS

CHEF'S TIP *I use chicken thighs instead of chicken breast because they hold up well for the extended cooking time and the results are moist and tender. You can substitute chicken breast here if you like, but the final results won't be quite as succulent.*

Roasted Pork Belly with Apples and Pears

Pork belly is an ultra-decadent cut of meat—the same cut that, when smoked, cured, and sliced, becomes heavenly bacon. When roasted whole, the crispy skin and the tender, soft meat make an incredibly mouthwatering and impressive dish.

¼ CUP (75 G) KOSHER SALT

¼ CUP (50 G) SUGAR

3 POUNDS (1365 G) PORK BELLY WITH SKIN

3 CLOVES GARLIC, THINLY SLICED

2 TABLESPOONS (30 ML) CANOLA OIL

2 APPLES

2 PEARS

1 TABLESPOON (15 ML) APPLE CIDER VINEGAR

1 TABLESPOON (11 G) WHOLE-GRAIN MUSTARD

SALT AND PEPPER TO TASTE

> ✕ **CHEF'S TIP** *Brining the meat isn't an essential step, but it's well worth the small amount of extra effort and planning because it ensures the most flavorful and moist results. You won't be disappointed.*

The night before you roast the pork, brine it to add flavor and tenderize the meat and keep it moist. Combine the salt and sugar in a bowl. Rub the mixture all over the pork belly, then refrigerate, covered, overnight. The meat will release some moisture as it sits.

The next day, remove it from the fridge, drain, rinse well, and pat dry.

Preheat the oven to 325°F (170°C, or gas mark 3).

Using a paring knife, score the skin on top of the pork belly by making diagonal slits through the fat, about 1 inch (2.5 cm) apart and ¼ inch (6 mm) deep. Turn over, and poke shallow holes into the meat with the tip of a paring knife, then stud these slits with the sliced garlic.

Heat a large sauté pan over medium-high heat. Add the canola oil, place the pork belly skin side down into the hot pan, and cook for 4 to 5 minutes to form a crisp, golden crust. Remove the pork belly from the sauté pan, place it in a roasting pan, crispy side up, and roast for 2 hours.

Remove the roasting pan from the oven and transfer the pork to a plate. Drain the excess fat from the pan. Core and chop the apples and pears into 1½-inch (3.8-cm) chunks and add them to the pan. Add the vinegar, mustard, and a pinch of salt and pepper to the fruit, and toss until evenly coated. Place the pork belly on top of apples and pears, and roast for 1 more hour, or until the meat is very tender.

Let rest, uncovered, for about 10 minutes. Slice the pork into thin strips and serve topped with the apples and pears.

◧ **YIELD: 4 SERVINGS**

Chilled Sesame Buckwheat Noodles

Buckwheat soba noodles are available in most stores. Be sure to check the label and ingredients to make sure it is 100 percent buckwheat. Some brands use a blend of wheat and buckwheat and are not gluten-free. This noodle recipe makes a great lunch or picnic option!

1	POUND (455 G) BUCKWHEAT SOBA NOODLES
2	CLOVES GARLIC, MINCED
1	TABLESPOON (8 G) GRATED GINGER
1	CUP (235 ML) CHICKEN STOCK OR WATER
3	TABLESPOONS (45 ML) RICE WINE VINEGAR OR WHITE WINE VINEGAR
3	TABLESPOONS (38 G) SUGAR
1	TEASPOON SALT
3	TABLESPOONS (45 G) TAHINI PASTE
6	TABLESPOONS (96 G) PEANUT BUTTER
2	TABLESPOONS (30 ML) SESAME OIL
3	TABLESPOONS (24 G) SESAME SEEDS
1	TEASPOON RED PEPPER FLAKES
4	SCALLIONS, THINLY SLICED
½	ENGLISH CUCUMBER, JULIENNED
3	CARROTS, JULIENNED

Fill a large stockpot three-fourths full with water, cover, and bring to a rapid boil over medium-high heat. Add the noodles and cook according to the time instructed on the package. Drain the noodles and rinse under cold water. Set aside.

In a large mixing bowl, combine the garlic, ginger, stock, vinegar, sugar, salt, tahini, peanut butter, and sesame oil. Whisk together until smooth. Add the noodles and toss to coat. Add the sesame seeds, red pepper flakes, scallion, cucumber, and carrots and toss to combine.

YIELD: 6 SERVINGS

CHEF'S TIPS *Buckwheat noodles tend to break if overcooked. Be sure to cook the noodles until just al dente—which usually takes just a few minutes—then stop the cooking by rinsing with cold water to avoid breakage.* ■ *If you are making this in advance, keep the ingredients chilled, but don't combine the noodles with the sauce until you are ready to serve. When you're ready to serve, bring the sauce to room temperature, then combine with the cold noodles. The sauce can get too thick if it is used right out of the refrigerator.*

Zucchini and Summer Squash Wrapped Salmon

These beautiful little packages of salmon make an extraordinary presentation without a huge effort. The salmon bakes in the oven but also steams in the vegetable wrapping, resulting in a moist and juicy fillet of fish.

6   BONELESS, SKINLESS SALMON FILLETS (ABOUT 2 POUNDS [910 G])

SALT AND PEPPER TO TASTE

3   CLOVES GARLIC, MINCED

3   TABLESPOONS (12 G) CHOPPED FRESH CHERVIL OR PARSLEY

3   TABLESPOONS (45 ML) LEMON JUICE

1   YELLOW SUMMER SQUASH

1   ZUCCHINI

3   TABLESPOONS (45 ML) OLIVE OIL

✂ CHEF'S TIP *Buying high-quality fresh fish is extremely important to a great-tasting dish. Fish fillets should smell like the sea, not fishy. They should be moist and shiny and firm to the touch, never mushy. When you buy fish and bring it home, use it as soon as you can, within 48 hours. Store the fish in the refrigerator in a plastic bag in a container of ice. The fish itself should not touch the ice.*

Preheat the oven to 350°F (180°C, or gas mark 4). Grease a baking sheet.

Season the fish generously with salt and pepper on both sides. Sprinkle with the chopped garlic, chervil, and lemon juice.

Cut the ends off of the squash and zucchini. Using a vegetable peeler, slice the vegetables into long, thin strips. You'll need 18 strips of each.

Overlap about 6 of the strips, alternating the zucchini and squash, on a flat surface. Place a piece of salmon on top. Wrap the ends of the zucchini and squash up and over the salmon to completely wrap the salmon. Repeat for each fillet.

Place the salmon on the prepared baking sheet, seam side down. Drizzle with the olive oil. Cover the baking sheet with aluminum foil and bake for 15 to 17 minutes, or until the salmon is cooked through.

▧ YIELD: 6 SERVINGS

Mussels with White Wine and Garlic

A simple garlic and white wine sauce meets its soul mate in sweet, tender mussels.
In a Belgian bistro these would be served with crispy, hot french fries. I like them with the
Truffled French Fries with Parmesan and Black Pepper on page 180.

2½ POUNDS (1138 G) CULTIVATED MUSSELS

1 TABLESPOON (14 G) UNSALTED BUTTER

5 CLOVES GARLIC, MINCED

1 SHALLOT, MINCED

1 CUP (235 ML) WHITE WINE

SALT AND PEPPER TO TASTE

¼ CUP (60 ML) HEAVY CREAM

2 TABLESPOONS (8 G) CHOPPED FRESH
CHERVIL OR PARSLEY

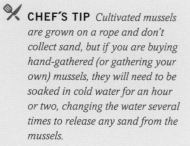

CHEF'S TIP *Cultivated mussels are grown on a rope and don't collect sand, but if you are buying hand-gathered (or gathering your own) mussels, they will need to be soaked in cold water for an hour or two, changing the water several times to release any sand from the mussels.*

Clean the mussels by scrubbing them with a stiff brush under cold water. If the beard (tough stringy bit that hangs off the side of the mussel) is still attached, pull it off with your fingers or a pair of pliers. If any of the mussels aren't shut tightly, tap them gently on the counter; if they close up, use them, and if they don't, discard them. Get rid of any mussels with cracked or broken shells.

In a large, heavy-bottomed stockpot, melt the butter over medium heat. Add the garlic and shallot and cook until tender and translucent, about 5 minutes. Add the white wine, increase the heat to high, and bring to a boil. Season generously with salt and pepper.

Add the mussels, cover the pot tightly, and cook for 6 to 8 minutes, or until all of the mussels open up. Add the cream and chopped chervil, toss to combine, and then transfer the mussels to a large bowl to serve. Serve with an empty bowl for the discarded shells.

YIELD: 4 SERVINGS

Roadside Tacos

This recipe is a complete one-eighty from the ground beef and crunchy taco shells of my childhood. These are full of fresh, vibrant flavor and are worth a bit of extra effort. You can use skirt or flank steak; boneless, skinless chicken breast or thighs; shrimp; or any white, flaky fish.

FOR TACOS:

2   TABLESPOONS (30 ML) OLIVE OIL

     ZEST AND JUICE OF 1 LIME

1   CANNED CHIPOTLE CHILE IN ADOBO SAUCE, CHOPPED, PLUS 2 TABLESPOONS (30 ML) ADOBO SAUCE

2   CLOVES GARLIC, MINCED

2   POUNDS (910 G) MEAT OR SEAFOOD OF YOUR CHOICE

18   SOFT CORN TORTILLAS, STORE-BOUGHT OR HOMEMADE (PAGE 176)

GARNISH SUGGESTIONS:

     CILANTRO

     DICED WHITE ONION

     FRESH CORN

     DICED TOMATOES

     CHOPPED JALAPEÑO

     QUESO FRESCO

     LIME WEDGES

     SALSA

     SWEET MANGO GUACAMOLE (PAGE 108)

To make the tacos: Combine the olive oil, lime zest and juice, chipotle chile and adobo sauce, and garlic in a large, shallow pan, add the meat, and marinate in the refrigerator for 2 hours. (Marinate fish or shrimp for only 30 minutes.)

Preheat the grill on high heat. This could also be done in a grill pan on the stove over high heat. If using skirt or flank steak, grill for about 2 minutes on each side for medium-rare. Chicken breast and boneless chicken thighs need about 5 minutes per side, depending on the thickness. For shrimp, it is easiest to skewer them and grill for 2 minutes per side. Fish will need about 3 minutes per side, depending on the thickness.

Thinly slice the steak or chicken, remove the shrimp from the skewers, or use a fork to pull the fish apart into large chunks.

If you have a gas range, warm the tortillas by heating them directly over a medium flame on your stove, just a few seconds per side. If you have an electric range, heat a small sauté pan over high heat, and warm them in the pan, a few seconds per side.

Assemble the tacos by placing a small amount of grilled protein into each of the corn tortillas and top with the desired garnishes.

YIELD: 6 SERVINGS

> **CHEF'S TIP** *Here are some of my favorite pairings. Feel free to mix them up as you like:*
> - *Steak tacos: Cilantro and onions*
> - *Shrimp tacos: Corn, jalapeños, and tomatoes*
> - *Chicken tacos: Queso fresco and salsa*
> - *Fish tacos: Shredded cabbage, scallion, and Sweet Mango Guacamole (page 108)*

Three Cheese Tomato and Eggplant Stacks

This fun take on eggplant Parmesan stacks layers of crispy eggplant with ripe tomatoes and melted cheese. Instead of tomato sauce, basil pesto is spread between each layer. Fresh is best, but in a pinch, use your favorite store-bought pesto.

1½ POUNDS (680 G) EGGPLANT

   SALT AND PEPPER TO TASTE

½ CUP (50 G) GRATED PARMESAN CHEESE

½ CUP (64 G) CORNSTARCH

1 TEASPOON GARLIC POWDER

2 EGGS

¼ CUP (60 ML) CANOLA OIL

½ CUP (125 G) RICOTTA CHEESE

½ CUP (60 G) SHREDDED MOZZARELLA CHEESE

½ CUP (130 G) BASIL PESTO (PAGE 179)

3 TOMATOES, SLICED INTO ½-INCH (1.3-CM) ROUNDS (YOU'LL NEED 12 SLICES TOTAL)

> ✗ **CHEF'S TIP** *Be sure to cook eggplant thoroughly to achieve a soft, creamy texture and best flavor. Undercooked eggplant is bitter and has an unpleasant spongy texture.*

Preheat the oven to 400°F (200°C, or gas mark 6).

Slice the eggplant into ½-inch (1.3-cm) slices. You will need 12 slices total. Season with salt and pepper.

In a medium bowl, combine the Parmesan, cornstarch, and garlic powder, and salt and pepper to taste. In a small bowl, lightly beat the eggs. Dip each eggplant slice into the egg, letting the excess drip back into the bowl, then coat evenly in the cornstarch mixture.

Heat the oil over medium heat in a large sauté pan or cast-iron skillet. When the oil is hot, fry the eggplant, a few slices at a time, for 3 to 4 minutes on each side, or until golden brown. Transfer to a wire rack to drain, and set aside.

In a small bowl, mix the ricotta and mozzarella together. Season with salt and pepper.

Assemble the stacks on a baking sheet. Place a slice of eggplant, a bit of the pesto, a slice of tomato, and a spoonful of the ricotta mixture. Repeat, then top with a final slice of eggplant. Make 3 more eggplant stacks the same way. Bake for 5 to 7 minutes, or until hot and the mozzarella is melted. Serve immediately.

◆ **YIELD: 4 SERVINGS**

Braised Ginger and Garlic Short Ribs

These hard-to-resist aromatic short ribs are a fantastic make-ahead meal that gets even better the next day. It's perfect with the Quinoa Pilaf with Roasted Root Vegetables on page 173.

3 POUNDS (1365 G) BONELESS SHORT RIBS (ABOUT 6 PIECES)

SALT AND PEPPER TO TASTE

3 TABLESPOONS (24 G) CORNSTARCH

1 TABLESPOON (15 ML) CANOLA OIL

½ CUP (120 ML) ORANGE JUICE (PREFERABLY FRESHLY SQUEEZED)

1 TABLESPOON (6 G) ORANGE ZEST

¼ CUP (60 ML) MIRIN

3 TABLESPOONS (45 ML) FISH SAUCE

1 CAN (14 OUNCES, OR 392 G) DICED TOMATOES

6 CLOVES GARLIC, MINCED

3 TABLESPOONS (24 G) GRATED GINGER

2 TABLESPOONS (30 G) BROWN SUGAR

¼ CUP (25 G) THINLY SLICED SCALLION

Preheat the oven to 300°F (150°C, or gas mark 2).

Heat a large, heavy-bottomed stockpot over high heat. Season the short ribs with salt and pepper, then dredge them in the cornstarch. Add the canola oil to the hot pan, then add the short ribs. Cook for 5 to 7 minutes, until golden brown, then turn and cook for another 5 to 7 minutes.

Add the orange juice and zest, mirin, fish sauce, diced tomatoes, garlic, ginger, and brown sugar to the pot. Bring to a boil, cover, and place the pot in the oven for 3 hours. The short ribs will become very tender and the sauce will thicken. Sprinkle with the scallions and serve.

To make in the slow cooker: Sear the short ribs as described above. Transfer to a 4- to 6-quart (3.6- to 5.4-L) slow cooker and add the orange juice and zest, mirin, fish sauce, diced tomatoes, garlic, ginger, and brown sugar. Cover and cook on high for 5 to 6 hours or on low for 7 to 8 hours. Sprinkle with the scallions and serve.

YIELD: 6 SERVINGS

CHEF'S TIP *Mirin is a sweet Japanese cooking condiment. You can usually find it in the international section of any grocery store, but you can substitute 1 part sugar and 1 part white wine or sake if you can't find it.*

mouthwatering **SIDES** *and*
ACCOMPANIMENTS

Creamed Spinach with Goat Cheese

*Goat cheese makes a brilliant upgrade to traditional creamed spinach.
Serve piled high atop grilled fillets of beef for a twist on a steakhouse favorite.*

1   TABLESPOON (15 ML) OLIVE OIL

4   CLOVES GARLIC, MINCED

2   POUNDS (910 G) BABY SPINACH

½   CUP (50 G) GRATED PARMESAN CHEESE

1   CUP (150 G) CRUMBLED GOAT CHEESE
    (ABOUT 4 OUNCES [112 G])

½   CUP (120 ML) CREAM

    SALT AND PEPPER TO TASTE

¼   TEASPOON FRESHLY GRATED NUTMEG
    (OPTIONAL)

Heat the olive oil in a large sauté pan over medium-high heat. Add the garlic and cook, stirring often, for 1 to 2 minutes, or until the garlic is golden brown around the edges and very fragrant.

Add the baby spinach and continue to cook, stirring often, until all of the spinach is wilted. Transfer the mixture to a colander set in the sink to drain. Press out as much moisture as you can.

Meanwhile, combine the Parmesan, goat cheese, and cream in the sauté pan. Stir to combine and melt the cheeses. Add the spinach back into the pan, and stir to coat with cheese mixture. Season to taste with salt, pepper, and nutmeg, if desired.

YIELD: 6 SERVINGS

Cayenne and Cinnamon Sweet Potato Wedges

These sweet potato wedges are sweet with a little hint of heat and are hard to resist. For more spice, add a little extra cayenne. These are made with no additional fat, so they are a guilt-free treat.

1½ POUNDS (680 G) SWEET POTATOES
    CUT INTO 1-INCH (2.5 CM) WEDGES

1   TABLESPOON (12 G) SUGAR

½   TEASPOON SALT

½   TEASPOON GROUND CINNAMON

⅛   TEASPOON GROUND CAYENNE

1   EGG WHITE, BEATEN

Preheat the oven to 350°F (180°C, or gas mark 4). Grease a non-stick or parchment-lined baking sheet.

In a small bowl, stir together the sugar, salt, and spices. Place the sweet potato wedges in a large bowl and add the egg white, tossing to coat. Sprinkle the spice mixture over to coat.

Place the potatoes, skin side down, on the prepared baking sheet and bake for 1 hour, or until golden and tender. If the sweet potatoes brown before they become tender, cover with aluminum foil and continue to bake until they are cooked through.

YIELD: 4 SERVINGS

Quinoa Pilaf with Roasted Root Vegetables

*Earthy and totally satisfying, this dish can be served as a side dish for meat,
or makes a fabulous vegetarian main course.*

2   CUPS (220 G) DICED ROOT VEGETABLES
    (ABOUT ½-INCH [1.3-CM] CUBES)

1   TABLESPOON (15 ML) PLUS 2 TEASPOONS
    OLIVE OIL, DIVIDED

    SALT AND PEPPER TO TASTE

2   CLOVES GARLIC, MINCED

½   ONION, DICED

1   CUP (173 G) QUINOA, RINSED

1½ CUPS (355 ML) CHICKEN STOCK OR
    WATER

> ✂ **CHEF'S TIP** *For the root veg-*
> *etables, use any combination of*
> *carrots, parsnips, turnips, beets,*
> *rutabaga, sweet potatoes, onions,*
> *celery root, and kohlrabi. Although*
> *they are all part of the same family*
> *of vegetables, each has a different*
> *flavor and texture to contribute to*
> *the dish.*

Preheat the oven to 375°F (190°C, or gas mark 5).

On a nonstick baking sheet or one lined with parchment paper, toss together the root vegetables, 2 teaspoons of the olive oil, and the salt and pepper. Bake for 20 minutes, or until the vegetables are tender and golden.

Meanwhile, in a medium saucepan, heat the remaining 1 tablespoon (15 ml) olive oil over medium heat. Add the garlic and onion and sauté until translucent, 5 minutes. Add the quinoa and stock and bring to a boil over medium-high heat. Cover, decrease the heat to a simmer, and cook for 20 minutes, or until the spiral-like germ has uncurled from the quinoa and it is tender. Remove from the heat and allow to rest for 10 minutes before tossing with a fork.

Stir in the roasted root vegetables. Season to taste with salt and pepper.

❄ **YIELD: 6 SERVINGS**

Baked Polenta with Oven-Roasted Tomatoes

Slowly roasting the tomatoes concentrates the flavor and makes them tangy and sweet.
Assemble this dish in advance, then just bake it when you need it.

6   PLUM TOMATOES

2   TABLESPOONS (30 ML) OLIVE OIL

2   TABLESPOONS (5 G) CHOPPED FRESH
    THYME OR ROSEMARY

    SALT AND PEPPER TO TASTE

4   CUPS (940 ML) CHICKEN STOCK OR
    WATER

1   CUP (140 G) YELLOW CORNMEAL, MEDIUM
    GRIND

1   CUP (100 G) GRATED PARMESAN CHEESE,
    DIVIDED

✗ CHEF'S TIP *Stir in shredded chicken or diced sausage when you add the 3/4 cup (75 g) Parmesan to the polenta for a hearty casserole that is a meal in itself.*

Preheat the oven to 300°F (150°C, or gas mark 2). Line a rimmed baking sheet with parchment paper. Grease a 9 x 13-inch (23 x 33-cm) baking dish.

Halve the tomatoes lengthwise, then place them, cut side up, on the prepared baking sheet. Sprinkle with the olive oil, thyme, and salt and pepper. Bake for 1½ hours, until the tomatoes shrivel and begin to caramelize.

When the tomatoes are almost done roasting, prepare the polenta. Bring the chicken stock to a boil in a stockpot over medium-high heat. Decrease the heat to medium and slowly whisk in the polenta; cook, stirring occasionally, for 20 minutes, or until the polenta is smooth and creamy, not gritty, when you taste it.

Season the polenta with salt and pepper and add ¾ cup (75 g) of the Parmesan cheese. Pour the polenta into the prepared baking dish and flatten the surface with an offset spatula. Press the roasted tomatoes into the polenta and sprinkle with remaining ¼ cup (25 g) Parmesan cheese.

Increase the oven temperature to 400°F (200°C, or gas mark 6) and bake for 20 minutes, or until the cheese is golden brown. Let cool slightly before slicing and serving.

■ YIELD: 8 SERVINGS

Handmade Chipotle and Cilantro Corn Tortillas

There is something truly special about homemade corn tortillas. The aroma, texture, and taste are unmatched by the store-bought alternative. You can find a cast-iron or an aluminum tortilla press at a kitchen supply store for about $20, and it makes quick work of shaping the tortillas, but if you don't have one, a rolling pin will do.

1¾ CUPS (220 G) MASA HARINA

1 CUP PLUS 2 TABLESPOONS (265 ML) LUKEWARM WATER (MORE IF NEEDED)

1 TABLESPOON (1 G) FINELY CHOPPED CILANTRO

½ CHIPOTLE PEPPER IN ADOBO, FINELY MINCED, PLUS 2 TABLESPOONS (30 ML) ADOBO SAUCE

PINCH OF SALT

CHEF'S TIP *Homemade tortillas are best served the same day. Here's a list of recipes where these delicious flatbreads make the perfect accompaniment:*
- *Spicy Refried Beans (pictured here; recipe on page 178)*
- *Huevos Rancheros (page 85)*
- *Sweet Mango Guacamole (page 108)*
- *Spicy Queso with Chorizo (page 108)*
- *Cuban Black Bean Soup with Avocado Crema (page 128)*
- *Steak Chili with Pickled Jalapeños and Butternut Squash (page 136)*
- *Roadside Tacos (page 167)*

Place the masa harina, water, cilantro, chipotle pepper, adobo sauce, and salt into a large bowl. Use your hands to knead the dough until it is soft, smooth, and malleable but not sticky. Roll the dough into golf ball–size balls and place on a plate. Cover with a damp paper towel to prevent the mixture from drying out.

Place a large sauté pan or cast-iron skillet over medium-high heat. Cut two 6-inch (15-cm) rounds from a heavy-duty (freezer) zipper-top plastic bag. If you don't have a tortilla press, place one plastic round on a flat surface, place a ball of the masa mixture in the center of the plastic, and top with the other piece of plastic. Use a rolling pin to roll a flat, round 5-inch (12.5-cm) tortilla. If using a tortilla press, place one piece of plastic on the bottom half of the tortilla press, then one dough ball in the center. Top with the second plastic round. Close the press, flattening the dough slightly, then rotate the dough in the plastic about 180 degrees, and press again to form a 5-inch (12.5-cm) round tortilla.

Peel off the top sheet of plastic. Hold the bottom layer of plastic and flip it over, transferring the tortilla to your other hand. Peel off the plastic and place the tortilla in the pan. Press down and add as many tortillas as will fit in your pan.

Cook the tortillas until they become dry at the edges and no longer stick to the skillet. Dark brown spots will begin to appear on the bottom of the tortilla after 1 to 2 minutes. Flip with a spatula and cook for another minute. Transfer the cooked tortillas to a plate and cover with a damp paper towel or plastic wrap.

Repeat with the remaining dough balls, stacking the cooked tortillas one on top of the other. The tortillas may seem brittle at first, but as they sit, they will become softer and more pliable. These will stay hot on your stove, covered, for 30 to 45 minutes.

YIELD: 14 TORTILLAS

Spicy Refried Beans

Traditionally, refried beans are made by frying mashed, cooked beans with lard. Here, I use just a little rendered bacon fat. For a lighter, vegetarian version, leave out the bacon. Serve with Roadside Tacos (page 167). See page 177 for photo of the dish (in a small blue bowl).

1	CUP (250 G) DRIED PINTO BEANS, PICKED THROUGH AND RINSED
5	CUPS (1175 ML) WATER OR CHICKEN STOCK
1	BAY LEAF
2	CLOVES GARLIC, MINCED
2	SLICES BACON, CHOPPED
½	ONION, MINCED
1	JALAPEÑO PEPPER, SEEDED AND MINCED
⅛	TEASPOON CAYENNE PEPPER
	SALT AND PEPPER TO TASTE

In a medium, heavy-bottomed pot, combine the dried beans, water, bay leaf, and garlic. Bring to a boil over medium heat, cover, decrease the heat to a simmer, and cook the beans for 2½ hours, or until very tender.

Drain the beans, reserving any remaining cooking liquid. In a large bowl, mash the beans with a potato masher or whisk.

Give the stockpot a quick rinse, then place it over medium heat and fry the bacon until it begins to get crispy. Add the onion and jalapeño. Sauté until the onion is translucent, about 5 minutes. Add the mashed beans and fry, stirring occasionally, for 3 to 5 minutes, adding a little bit of the reserved cooking liquid if needed to make the beans creamy.

Season to taste with cayenne, salt, and pepper, and serve.

YIELD: 6 SERVINGS

CHEF'S TIP *To cut down on cooking time, soak the beans in cold water overnight. Drain, rinse, and follow the recipe above, but cook for about 50 minutes, or until very tender.*

Grilled Asparagus with Basil Pesto

Asparagus is one of the quickest and simplest veggies to prepare. An indoor grill or an outdoor charcoal or gas grill works well to cook the asparagus. A traditional Italian pesto livens up this familiar veggie with the vibrant flavor of fresh basil.

FOR BASIL PESTO:

1   CLOVE GARLIC

1   TABLESPOON (9 G) PINE NUTS

2   TABLESPOONS (10 G) GRATED PARMESAN CHEESE

½   CUP (20 G) PACKED FRESH BASIL LEAVES, RINSED AND PATTED DRY

¼   CUP (60 ML) EXTRA-VIRGIN OLIVE OIL

FOR ASPARAGUS:

2   BUNCHES ASPARAGUS

1   TEASPOON OLIVE OIL

    SALT AND PEPPER TO TASTE

To make the pesto: Place the garlic clove in a food processor (a mini food processor works well here) and pulse to finely chop. Add the pine nuts, grated Parmesan cheese, and basil. Pulse again until the basil is finely chopped. Add the extra-virgin olive oil and process until you have a thick sauce (it should have some texture to it, but not any large pieces of pine nuts visible). The pesto can be made in advance, but let it come to room temperature before serving it with the asparagus. Set the pesto aside.

To make the asparagus: Preheat a grill on high. Cut the tough, white bottoms off of the asparagus (the bottom 2 to 3 inches [5 to 7.5 cm]). Toss the asparagus spears with the olive oil and a sprinkle of salt and pepper.

Grill the asparagus for 3 to 4 minutes, or until slightly charred and the spears are tender but still crisp. There is no need to turn them. Transfer to a plate and spoon the pesto over the spears. Serve immediately.

▮ YIELD: 6 SERVINGS

CHEF'S TIP *Don't have a grill? Place the asparagus on a baking sheet and place under the broiler for 3 to 4 minutes.*

VARIATION *Try using cilantro or a combination of your favorite herbs in place of the basil for a new kind of pesto.*

Truffled French Fries with Parmesan and Black Pepper

Twice cooking the potatoes ensures that they are cooked through and crisp and golden on the outside without over-browning. A few simple additions make these fabulous, but not fussy.

3   LARGE RUSSET POTATOES

4   CUPS (940 ML) CANOLA OR PEANUT OIL, FOR FRYING

    SALT AND PEPPER TO TASTE

2   TABLESPOONS (30 ML) TRUFFLE OIL

¼   CUP (25 G) GRATED PARMESAN CHEESE

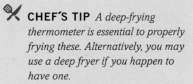

CHEF'S TIP *A deep-frying thermometer is essential to properly frying these. Alternatively, you may use a deep fryer if you happen to have one.*

Cut the potatoes into long sticks ¼ inch (6 mm) thick. Preheat the oil to 300°F (150°C) in a large sauté pan or cast-iron skillet. Fry the potatoes for 5 to 7 minutes, or until tender. Drain on a wire rack or a plate lined with paper towels. Let cool for 10 minutes or up to 2 hours.

Heat the oil to 350°F (180°C). Fry again, for about 3 minutes, or until golden brown. Drain and immediately sprinkle with salt and lots of coarse freshly ground pepper. Drizzle the truffle oil over the fries, then toss them to evenly coat them with the seasonings. Sprinkle with the Parmesan cheese and serve.

YIELD: 6 SERVINGS

Classic Ratatouille

This classic French dish combines fresh summer vegetables with garlic, olive oil, and herbs. The vegetables are added one at a time, starting with the ones that take the longest to cook and ending with the ones requiring the shortest cooking time, to ensure that all of the vegetables are tender, but not mushy, when the dish is completed.

2   TABLESPOONS (30 ML) OLIVE OIL

1   ONION, DICED

4   CLOVES GARLIC, MINCED

1   POUND (455 G) EGGPLANT, DICED

1   RED BELL PEPPER, STEMMED, SEEDED, AND DICED

1   GREEN BELL PEPPER, STEMMED, SEEDED, AND DICED

1   POUND (455 G) ZUCCHINI, DICED

1   POUND (455 G) SUMMER SQUASH, DICED

2   TOMATOES, DICED

2   TEASPOONS FRESH THYME LEAVES

SALT AND PEPPER TO TASTE

In a large, heavy-bottomed pot, heat the olive oil over medium heat. Add the onion and garlic and cook until softened, about 5 minutes.

Add the eggplant and cook for 5 minutes, until it begins to soften, stirring only occasionally. Add the bell peppers and cook for another 2 to 3 minutes. Add the zucchini, summer squash, and tomatoes and cook for 4 to 5 minutes, stirring now and then, until all of the vegetables are just tender. Remove from the heat, add the fresh thyme, season with salt and pepper, and serve.

YIELD: 6 SERVINGS

CHEF'S TIP *Ratatouille is the perfect side, and it is also delicious as a filling for an omelet, as a bed for poached eggs, spooned over soft polenta, or stirred into a risotto!*

Cumin-Scented Black Bean and Cucumber Salad

This salad is refreshing and filling and is perfect on hot days when you do not want to turn on the stove or the oven. I love to pack it along for a picnic lunch.

1   CLOVE GARLIC, MINCED

1   TABLESPOON (15 ML) OLIVE OIL

2   TABLESPOONS (30 ML) LEMON OR LIME JUICE

¼   TEASPOON GROUND CUMIN

PINCH OF RED PEPPER FLAKES (OPTIONAL)

SALT AND PEPPER TO TASTE

1½   CUPS (384 G) COOKED BLACK BEANS OR 1 CAN (15 OUNCES, OR 420 G), DRAINED AND RINSED

1   CUP (120 G) DICED SEEDLESS CUCUMBER

1   CUP (180 G) DICED SEEDED TOMATO

¼   CUP (25 G) THINLY SLICED SCALLION (WHITE AND GREEN PARTS)

In a medium bowl, make the dressing by whisking together the garlic, olive oil, lemon juice, cumin, red pepper flakes, and salt and pepper until combined.

In a large bowl, combine the black beans, cucumber, tomato, and scallion. Pour in the dressing and toss until well mixed. This is best after it has been chilled in the refrigerator for at least 1 hour so the flavors have a chance to combine, but it can be served immediately if desired.

YIELD: 6 SERVINGS

CHEF'S TIP *I always prefer beans that I've cooked myself rather than the canned variety. To save time, I make a big pot of beans, then freeze them in 11/2-cup (384-g) portions in plastic zipper-top bags. Each bag equals the equivalent of one 15-ounce (420-g) can of beans.*

Potatoes au Gratin with Gruyère and Nutmeg

Also known as scalloped potatoes, potatoes au gratin is simply thinly sliced potatoes layered with cheese and milk and baked until tender, golden, and delicious. I use a combination of sweet potatoes and waxy potatoes, but you can use just one or the other.

2½ **POUNDS (1138 G) POTATOES**

SALT AND PEPPER TO TASTE

FRESHLY GRATED NUTMEG TO TASTE

6 **OUNCES (168 G) GRUYÈRE CHEESE, GRATED**

1¼ **CUPS (295 ML) MILK**

> **CHEF'S TIPS** *Waxy potatoes are the smaller round potatoes with yellow or red skin. They are lower in starch than the oblong gray-brown russet potatoes and are perfect for this dish because they bake up creamy and tender. ■ Nutmeg is a traditional spice used in combination with cheese or cream sauces and is the perfect complement to potatoes au gratin. Just remember, a little goes a long way, so use it sparingly. Always grate your nutmeg fresh for best flavor (you can use a microplane).*

Preheat the oven to 350°F (180°C, or gas mark 4). Grease a 9 x 9-inch (23 x 23-cm) baking dish.

Peel and slice the potatoes into ¼-inch (6-mm) slices. A mandolin or slicer attachment on your food processor will make quick work of the slicing.

Place one layer of potatoes in the dish and season with a sprinkle of salt, pepper, and nutmeg, then some of the Gruyère cheese. Repeat until all of the potatoes are used up. When you get to the last layer of potato, season with salt, pepper, and nutmeg, then pour in the milk. Press down on the potato slices until you see the milk rise up along the edges of the baking dish to evenly distribute the milk. Top with the remaining Gruyère, cover tightly with foil, and bake for 1 hour. Remove the foil and bake for another 15 minutes, or until the top is golden and the edges bubble.

Let cool slightly before slicing and serving.

■ **YIELD: 8 SERVINGS**

Roasted Brussels Sprouts with Bacon and Onions

One pan and 20 minutes is all it takes to make this yummy dish. I love brussels sprouts, and this is my favorite way to serve them!

1   POUND (455 G) BRUSSELS SPROUTS,
     ENDS TRIMMED, THEN CUT IN HALF

4   SLICES BACON, DICED

½   CUP (80 G) DICED WHITE ONION

     SALT AND PEPPER TO TASTE

Preheat the oven to 400°F (200°C, or gas mark 6).

Place the brussels sprouts, diced bacon, white onion, and a sprinkle of salt and pepper on a rimmed baking sheet. Stir to combine.

Roast for 20 minutes, stirring once halfway through to promote even browning. Serve hot.

◆ YIELD: 4 SERVINGS

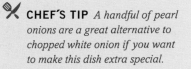

CHEF'S TIP *A handful of pearl onions are a great alternative to chopped white onion if you want to make this dish extra special.*

Sautéed Kale and Apples

Enough cannot be said about the goodness of kale. It is rich in nutrients and an excellent source of vitamins K, C, and A, among many others. Kale is a cruciferous vegetable that is a known cancer fighter, detoxifier, and anti-inflammatory.

1   TABLESPOON (15 ML) OLIVE OIL

½   ONION, THINLY SLICED

1   APPLE, CORED AND THINLY SLICED

1   BUNCH KALE, STEMS REMOVED, CHOPPED INTO BITE-SIZE PIECES

2   TABLESPOONS (30 ML) WATER

1   TABLESPOON (15 ML) APPLE CIDER VINEGAR

    SALT AND PEPPER TO TASTE

In a large skillet, heat the olive oil over medium heat. Add the onion and apple and sauté until softened, about 5 minutes.

Add the kale and water, cover, and cook until the kale is wilted and tender, about 5 minutes. Stir in the apple cider vinegar and season with salt and pepper to taste.

YIELD: 4 SERVINGS

CHEF'S TIP *The stems of kale are tough. For a quick sauté like this, it's best to remove them because they don't cook long enough to get tender. Hold the kale by the stem in one hand, then run your other hand briskly along the stem to the leaf tip to remove the stem.*

Molasses Baked Beans

Smoky, sweet baked beans are a classic! This version uses lots of robust, bittersweet molasses. This method does not require overnight soaking of the beans.

5	SLICES BACON, CHOPPED
1	ONION, DICED
4	CLOVES GARLIC, DICED
2	BAY LEAVES
6	CUPS (1410 ML) WATER
2	CUPS (500 G) WHITE BEANS, PINTO BEANS, OR BLACK BEANS
2	TABLESPOONS (22 G) DIJON MUSTARD
1	CUP (240 G) KETCHUP
¼	CUP (60 ML) APPLE CIDER VINEGAR
½	CUP (170 G) MOLASSES
1	TEASPOON GARLIC POWDER
1	TEASPOON ONION POWDER
	SALT AND PEPPER TO TASTE

Preheat the oven to 325°F (170°C, or gas mark 3).

In a large, heavy-bottomed, oven safe stockpot or Dutch oven, sauté the bacon over medium heat until the fat is rendered and it just begins to get crispy, about 5 minutes. Add the onion, garlic, bay leaves, water, and beans, stir to combine, cover, and bring to a simmer. Place the pot in the oven and cook for 2 hours.

Add the Dijon mustard, ketchup, apple cider vinegar, molasses, garlic powder, onion powder, and salt and pepper and stir to combine. Cover and bake for another 2 hours, or until the beans are tender and the sauce has thickened. Season to taste with salt and pepper.

YIELD: 8 SERVINGS

> ✕ **CHEF'S TIP** *Canned beans can be used in place of dried for a quicker version of this recipe. Use three 15-ounce (420-g) cans, drained. Add the Dijon mustard, ketchup, apple cider vinegar, molasses, garlic powder, onion powder, salt, and pepper and bake for 30 to 45 minutes.*

Maple and Orange Sweet Potato Mash

A touch of orange and maple are the perfect complement to this silky sweet potato purée.

2   LARGE SWEET POTATOES (ABOUT 2
     POUNDS [910 G] TOTAL)

¼   CUP (60 ML) MAPLE SYRUP

½   CUP (120 ML) MILK

¼   CUP (60 ML) FRESHLY SQUEEZED ORANGE
     JUICE

2   TEASPOONS ORANGE ZEST

     SALT AND PEPPER TO TASTE

CHEF'S TIP *The food processor
makes this dish silky smooth. If
you like a little more texture, first
mash the sweet potatoes in a bowl
with a fork, then add the remaining
ingredients and stir by hand.*

Preheat the oven to 350°F (180°C, or gas mark 4).

Pierce the sweet potatoes with a fork and place them on a baking sheet. Bake for about 1 hour, or until easily pierced with a fork. Cut the potatoes in half and then let cool for 5 to 10 minutes, or until cool enough to handle.

Add the maple syrup, milk, orange juice, orange zest, and a pinch of salt and pepper to the bowl of a food processor. Scoop the flesh of the sweet potatoes into the bowl, discarding the skins. Put the lid on the food processor and pulse until smooth and creamy. Season again with salt and pepper if needed. Transfer to a serving dish and serve.

YIELD: 6 SERVINGS

Parmesan Roasted Broccoli

Roasting is one of the simplest and most delicious ways to prepare broccoli, because it caramelizes and concentrates the flavor. This is a great side dish for almost any main course.

1½ **POUNDS (680 G) BROCCOLI FLORETS**

2 **TABLESPOONS (30 ML) OLIVE OIL**

  SALT AND PEPPER TO TASTE

¼ **CUP (25 G) PARMESAN CHEESE**

1 **TABLESPOON (6 G) LEMON ZEST**

Preheat the oven to 400°F (200°C, or gas mark 6). Line a baking sheet with parchment paper.

On the prepared baking sheet, toss together the broccoli, olive oil, and salt and pepper. Spread out the broccoli florets in a single layer. Sprinkle the Parmesan cheese and lemon zest evenly over the top.

Bake for 20 minutes, or until the cheese is golden and the florets are crisp.

YIELD: 4 SERVINGS

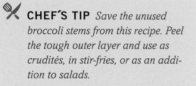

CHEF'S TIP *Save the unused broccoli stems from this recipe. Peel the tough outer layer and use as crudités, in stir-fries, or as an addition to salads.*

Chapter

9

DIVINE DESSERTS

Boozy Butterscotch Pudding

This pudding has just enough whiskey to give it a kick without overpowering the sweet and salty caramel flavors. I served this dessert at my last holiday cocktail party in shot glasses, which made for perfect portions for mingling.

1   CUP (225 G) UNSALTED BUTTER

1⅔ CUPS (374 G) LIGHTLY PACKED DARK BROWN SUGAR

4   CUPS (940 ML) WHOLE MILK

5   TABLESPOONS (40 G) CORNSTARCH

3   WHOLE EGGS PLUS 1 EGG YOLK

1   TEASPOON SALT

1   TABLESPOON (15 ML) VANILLA EXTRACT

¼   CUP (60 ML) WHISKEY OR DARK RUM

 CHEF'S TIP *I always make sure my garnish does more than just decorate. The color, flavor, and texture of your garnish should always complement the dish. In this instance, an airy dollop of unsweetened whipped cream or a bit of shaved dark chocolate would be the perfect contrast to the velvety sweet pudding.*

Melt the butter in a large, heavy-bottomed saucepan over medium heat. Once the butter is completely melted, add the brown sugar and stir to combine. Whisk in the milk, cornstarch, whole eggs and egg yolk, and salt. Continue to cook over medium heat, whisking often, for 10 to 15 minutes, or until the pudding just begins to thicken. At this point, decrease the heat slightly to medium-low. Continue whisking until the pudding is thick enough that it coats the back of a spoon and doesn't run when you swipe your finger down the center of the spoon.

Remove from the heat. Whisk in the vanilla and rum. Set a fine-mesh strainer over a large bowl. Pour the pudding through the strainer to remove any lumps that may have formed while cooking. Lay a sheet of plastic wrap directly on top of the pudding (this will prevent a skin from forming) and refrigerate until cold, 3 to 4 hours. Spoon the pudding into individual serving dishes, and serve with the garnish of your choice (see Chef's Tip left).

YIELD: 8 SERVINGS

Prosecco Zabaglione with Strawberries and Peaches

Traditionally made with Marsala wine, zabaglione is a deliciously simple, airy custard served with fruit or cake. Here, I serve it with strawberries and peaches, two fruits that complement the Prosecco beautifully.

⅔ CUP (160 ML) HEAVY CREAM

4 EGG YOLKS

⅓ CUP (65 G) SUGAR

1 TEASPOON FRESHLY GRATED ORANGE ZEST

½ CUP (120 ML) PROSECCO SPARKLING WINE

2 CUPS (290 G) STRAWBERRIES, STEMMED AND QUARTERED

2 RIPE PEACHES, PITTED AND SLICED

CHEF'S TIP *That's a lot of whisking! When I've already had my workout for the day, I make this using a handheld electric mixer instead of a whisk.*

Beat the heavy cream in a large bowl until stiff peaks form. Refrigerate until ready to use.

Place 2 inches (5 cm) of water in a saucepan and bring to a simmer. Place a metal or glass bowl on top of the saucepan (it should not touch the water) and add the egg yolks, sugar, orange zest, and Prosecco. Whisk vigorously until pale and thick, 5 to 7 minutes.

Fill another large bowl with ice water. Place the egg yolk mixture over the bowl of ice water and continue whisking until the zabaglione is cool, another 5 to 7 minutes. Gently fold in the whipped cream.

Layer the zabaglione into 6 glasses with the strawberries and peaches. Serve chilled.

YIELD: 6 SERVINGS

Chocolate Peanut Butter Fondue

This sinfully delicious fondue is as much for the peanut butter lovers as it is for the chocoholics. Serve in a fondue pot to keep warm if you have one, or if eaten right away, it will stay soft enough for dipping right out of a bowl.

½   CUP (120 ML) HEAVY CREAM
½   CUP (120 ML) MILK
½   CUP (130 G) PEANUT BUTTER
1   TEASPOON VANILLA EXTRACT
4   OUNCES (115 G) DARK CHOCOLATE CHIPS

In a medium saucepan, combine the cream and milk and bring to a simmer over medium heat. Add the peanut butter and vanilla and whisk until smooth.

Remove from the heat and add the chocolate chips. Whisk until the chips have melted. Serve.

YIELD: 6 SERVINGS

CHEF'S TIP *Serve with lots of fresh fruit for dipping. I like bananas and strawberries, but get creative and try potato chips, dried fruits, marshmallows, crispy rice squares (just make sure your crispy rice cereal doesn't contain malt!), or even the Five-Ingredient PB&J Cookies on page 210!*

Buttermilk Panna Cotta with Balsamic Fruit Salsa

Panna cotta in Italian literally means "cooked cream." This version includes tangy buttermilk. These soft, creamy Italian custards can be made up to two days in advance and stored covered in the refrigerator. The fruit salsa should be made an hour or two before serving.

FOR PANNA COTTA:

2   TABLESPOONS (30 ML) WATER

1   TABLESPOON (8 G) UNFLAVORED POWDERED GELATIN

1   CUP (235 ML) HEAVY CREAM

½   CUP (100 G) SUGAR

2   CUPS (470 ML) BUTTERMILK, SHAKEN

1   TABLESPOON (15 ML) VANILLA EXTRACT

FOR FRUIT SALSA:

¾   CUP (128 G) DICED STRAWBERRIES

¾   CUP (124 G) DICED PLUMS OR NECTARINES

2   TABLESPOONS (30 ML) AGED BALSAMIC VINEGAR

1   TABLESPOON (12 G) SUGAR

To make the panna cotta: Lightly grease six 1-cup (235-ml) ramekins.

Place the water in a small bowl and sprinkle the gelatin over the surface. Allow to sit for 5 to 10 minutes to "bloom," or hydrate, the gelatin.

In a medium saucepan, combine the cream and sugar over medium heat and cook until the sugar has dissolved, 2 to 3 minutes. Remove from the heat and stir in the gelatin. Stir to dissolve the gelatin, about 2 minutes. Add the buttermilk and vanilla, and stir to combine. Divide the mixture evenly among the prepared ramekins. Chill for at least 4 hours, or until set.

To make the fruit salsa: Combine the strawberries, plums, balsamic vinegar, and sugar in a medium bowl. Let the fruit macerate, stirring occasionally, until the sugar has dissolved and the fruit begins to release its juices, about 20 minutes.

To serve, run a knife along the edge of the ramekins to loosen the panna cotta. Invert the ramekin onto a plate, then remove the ramekin to unmold. Spoon the fruit salsa and juices on top. Serve cold.

YIELD: 6 SERVINGS

CHEF'S TIP *Lesser-quality balsamic is aged in steel tanks, has added water, and has added brown sugar or caramel to deepen the color. The best balsamic vinegar is aged in wooden barrels the traditional way, in and around a small area of Modena, Italy. Use the best quality that's in your budget.*

Bittersweet Chocolate Pots de Crème

Pot de crème, or "pot of cream," is simply a rich, baked custard. Traditionally, these were served in small lidded pots, but ramekins work well here. I go crazy for bananas, so I pair this with a banana whipped cream (page 200), but see the variations listed there for some other delicious choices as well.

5 EGG YOLKS

¼ CUP (50 G) SUGAR

½ VANILLA BEAN

1 CUP (235 ML) MILK

1½ CUPS (355 ML) HEAVY CREAM

4 OUNCES (115 G) BITTERSWEET CHOCOLATE, FINELY CHOPPED

CHEF'S TIP *For a dairy-free pot de crème, substitute equal parts coconut milk for the milk and cream in this recipe.*

Preheat the oven to 350°F (180°C, or gas mark 4).

In a medium bowl, whisk together the egg yolks and sugar until well combined. Set aside.

Use a paring knife to split open the length of the vanilla bean. Use the back of the knife (the dull side) to scrape the seeds out of the vanilla bean pod and into a heavy-bottomed saucepan. Add the scraped vanilla pod, milk, and cream to the saucepan. Place the pan over medium heat and slowly bring the mixture to a boil. Be sure to watch the pot because milk and cream will quickly boil over!

Remove the milk mixture from the heat and add the chopped chocolate. Let it sit for 1 minute to let the chocolate begin to melt, then whisk until the chocolate is completely melted and the mixture is smooth.

Remove the chocolate mixture from the heat and stream it very slowly into the egg yolk mixture, whisking as you go to combine. Be careful not to add the hot milk too quickly or you will cook the eggs.

Pour the mixture through a fine-mesh strainer into another bowl. Ladle the mixture into six ¾-cup (180-ml) ramekins. Place the ramekins inside a large baking dish, such as a lasagna pan. Fill the baking dish with hot water about halfway up the sides of the ramekins (this is so the pots de crème cook slowly and evenly). Place the baking dish in the oven and bake for 30 minutes, or until the center of each custard is set but still jiggles slightly when you jostle it.

Cool the custards to room temperature, then cover with plastic wrap and refrigerate until ready to serve (at least 2 to 3 hours but up to 3 days).

YIELD: 6 SERVINGS

Banana Whipped Cream

This simple, lightly sweet whipped cream is the perfect topping for fresh berries and makes an easy icing for cakes or cupcakes. But my favorite way to serve it is with anything chocolate: dolloped into hot cocoa or as the crowning glory for my Chocolate Pots de Crème on page 198.

1 LARGE RIPE BANANA

¾ CUP (180 ML) HEAVY CREAM

1 TABLESPOON (8 G) POWDERED SUGAR

Place the peeled banana into the bowl of a food processor (a mini food processor works great) and process until smooth and creamy, about 30 seconds.

Place the heavy cream and powdered sugar in a bowl. Beat with an electric mixer on high speed for 2 to 3 minutes, or until the cream forms stiff peaks. Use a rubber spatula to gently fold the banana purée into the whipped cream until completely incorporated. This will store well, chilled, for several hours.

YIELD: 6 SERVINGS

CHEF'S TIP *For a dairy-free "whipped cream," replace the heavy cream with silken tofu, then process all ingredients together in a mini food processor until smooth and creamy.*

VARIATIONS *For raspberry whipped cream, omit the banana and fold 1 to 2 tablespoons (20 to 40 g) raspberry jam into the whipped cream.* ■ *For chocolate whipped cream, omit the banana and add 1 additional tablespoon (8 g) powdered sugar and 1 tablespoon (8 g) cocoa powder to the heavy cream before whipping.*

Raspberry Soufflé

Soufflés seem fancy-shmancy but are really pretty easy! Prepare and chill the raspberry mixture in advance, then right before you are ready for dessert, just whip the egg whites, fold in the raspberry mixture, and bake. Tart and light as air, this soufflé makes the perfect finale to a rich, heavy meal.

1 **CUP (200 G) SUGAR, DIVIDED**

2 **CUPS (250 G) FRESH RASPBERRIES**

4 **TEASPOONS (10 G) CORNSTARCH**

¼ **CUP (60 ML) CREAM, CHILLED**

4 **EGGS, SEPARATED**

1 **TABLESPOON (8 G) POWDERED SUGAR (OPTIONAL)**

✗ **CHEF'S TIP** *Resist the temptation to open the oven during baking. Opening the oven can cause a sudden drop in the temperature of the oven and the soufflés can fall!*

Preheat the oven to 350°F (180°C, or gas mark 4). Grease six ¾-cup (180-ml) ramekins, and use ¼ cup (50 g) of the sugar to coat the insides of the ramekins. Pour out any excess sugar.

Place the raspberries and the remaining ¾ cup (150 g) sugar in a small saucepan over medium heat. Cook for 10 minutes to dissolve the sugar and cook the raspberries until they release their juices and turn to mush. Remove from the heat and strain through a fine-mesh strainer. Press the pulp with the back of a spoon to push the juice and pulp through the strainer, leaving only the seeds behind.

Discard the seeds and place the raspberry purée back in the saucepan. Whisk together the cornstarch and the cold cream and add it to the pan. Cook over medium heat, stirring occasionally, until it just begins to bubble. The mixture will thicken. Remove from the heat and whisk in the egg yolks 1 at a time. Refrigerate until cold, at least 1 hour; the mixture will thicken even more.

In a separate clean bowl, beat the egg whites to stiff peaks. Fold about one-fourth of the whipped egg whites into the raspberry mixture to aerate the raspberry purée, then gently fold the purée into the egg whites.

Spoon into the prepared ramekins (fill them to the very top) and place on a rimmed baking sheet. Bake in the middle of the oven for 16 to 18 minutes. The soufflés are done when they have puffed high over the rim, the top just begins to turn golden, and the center still jiggles slightly.

To garnish, place the powdered sugar in a small fine-mesh sieve. Shake the sieve over the soufflés to dust them with the sugar. Serve right away, because the soufflés will deflate after a few minutes.

▌ **YIELD: 6 SERVINGS**

Thai Coconut Sticky Rice with Mango

Perfectly ripe, sweet mango is the key to success in this recipe. Mangoes should be heavy for their size, be sweet smelling, and give a bit when pressed with your thumb. Combined with creamy, salty, and sweet jasmine rice, this is an irresistible, exotic dessert.

1   CUP (190 G) JASMINE RICE

1½ CUPS (355 ML) WATER

1   TEASPOON SALT

½   CUP (100 G) SUGAR

1   CUP (235 ML) COCONUT MILK

2   MANGOES, PEELED, SEEDED, AND SLICED

1   TABLESPOON (8 G) SESAME SEEDS

> ✕ **CHEF'S TIP** *Jasmine rice is sometimes called fragrant rice. To make the perfect tender rice, it is important to use gentle heat, just simmering. Use a pot with a tight-fitting lid, and leave the rice alone while it is cooking. Do not uncover or stir until it is finished.*

Place the jasmine rice in a fine sieve and rinse under cold water for 1 minute, or until the water runs clear. In a medium saucepan, combine the rice and water and bring to a boil over medium heat. Cover the saucepan, decrease the heat to low, and simmer for 20 minutes, or until the rice is tender and all of the water has been absorbed. Do not stir.

In the meantime, in a small saucepan, combine the salt, sugar, and coconut milk. Cook over medium heat, stirring occasionally, until the sugar dissolves. Remove from the heat and set aside.

Once the rice is cooked, transfer to a large bowl. Reserve and set aside ¼ cup (60 ml) of the coconut milk mixture. Pour the remaining ¾ cup (180 ml) coconut milk mixture over the rice, cover with plastic wrap, and let sit until it has cooled to room temperature and the coconut milk has absorbed into the rice.

Divide the sliced mango among 4 plates. Drizzle the mango with the reserved coconut milk mixture and garnish with the sesame seeds. Spoon the sticky rice onto the plates alongside the mango and serve at room temperature.

◼ **YIELD: 4 SERVINGS**

Ultra-Moist Cornmeal Upside-Down Cake

Pineapple upside-down cake is a classic recipe that tugs on the heartstrings, reminding many of home.
This incredibly moist and flavorful version is made with cornmeal, which adds a distinct texture.
Serve with a dollop of freshly whipped cream.

FOR TOPPING:

¼ CUP (55 G) UNSALTED BUTTER

¾ CUP (170 G) PACKED DARK BROWN SUGAR

9 SLICES CANNED PINEAPPLE, PLUS ½ CUP (120 ML) PINEAPPLE JUICE, RESERVED FOR CAKE BATTER

FOR CAKE:

⅓ CUP (80 ML) CANOLA OIL

2 EGGS

¼ CUP (60 G) PLAIN YOGURT, STORE-BOUGHT OR HOMEMADE (PAGE 77)

1 TABLESPOON (15 ML) VANILLA EXTRACT

¾ CUP (150 G) GRANULATED SUGAR

1 CUP (83 G) GROUND ALMOND FLOUR (MADE FROM ABOUT ¾ CUP [83 G] ALMONDS, SEE CHEF'S TIP)

¾ CUP (105 G) CORNMEAL

2 TABLESPOONS (16 G) CORNSTARCH

1 TEASPOON BAKING POWDER

½ TEASPOON BAKING SODA

¼ TEASPOON SALT

Preheat the oven to 350°F (180°C, or gas mark 4). Generously grease a 9 x 9 inch (23 x 23-cm) baking pan.

To make the topping: In a small saucepan over medium heat, melt the butter and the brown sugar until all the sugar has dissolved. Pour into the greased pan and then arrange the pineapple slices on top of that. Set aside.

To make the cake: In a large mixing bowl, combine the oil, eggs, yogurt, vanilla, and reserved pineapple juice. Whisk until well combined.

In a separate mixing bowl, combine the granulated sugar, almond flour, cornmeal, cornstarch, baking powder, baking soda, and salt. Whisk to combine. Stir the dry ingredients into the wet until well incorporated. Pour over the pineapple slices, and bake for 45 minutes, or until the middle is set.

Let the cake cool in the pan on a cooling rack for 1 hour before inverting onto a platter.

YIELD: 9 SERVINGS

+ VARIATION *Substitute 2 cups (290 g) fresh berries for the pineapple in the topping, and substitute apple or orange juice for the pineapple juice in the batter to make a berry upside-down cake.*

✕ CHEF'S TIP *You can find almond flour (which is finer than packaged almond meal) at specialty stores, but it can be expensive and difficult to locate. Make your own almond flour by grinding raw or blanched almonds in a food processor. Pulse several times until the almonds are finely ground. (Don't over-grind because you can wind up with almond butter!) Pour the ground almonds through a fine-mesh sieve over a bowl. Use your fingers to coax the almonds through the sieve, leaving behind any larger pieces. Put the larger pieces back in the food processor, and repeat the process until all the almonds are finely ground. Store any leftover flour in the refrigerator or freezer.*

Clementine and Honey Cake

Almost like a pudding cake, this dessert has an amazing custardlike texture with a burst of orange flavor. If clementines aren't available, substitute oranges, and boil for an additional 30 minutes. Serve with soft whipped cream.

1   POUND (455 G) CLEMENTINES (ABOUT 6)

2   CUPS (166 G) ALMOND FLOUR (SEE CHEF'S TIP ON PAGE 204)

2   TEASPOONS BAKING POWDER

5   EGGS

1   CUP (200 G) SUGAR

1   TABLESPOON (15 ML) VANILLA EXTRACT

¼   CUP (55 G) UNSALTED BUTTER, MELTED

½   CUP (175 G) HONEY

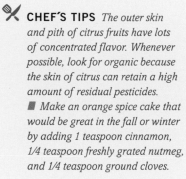

CHEF'S TIPS *The outer skin and pith of citrus fruits have lots of concentrated flavor. Whenever possible, look for organic because the skin of citrus can retain a high amount of residual pesticides.*

■ Make an orange spice cake that would be great in the fall or winter by adding 1 teaspoon cinnamon, 1/4 teaspoon freshly grated nutmeg, and 1/4 teaspoon ground cloves.

Bring a large pot of water to a boil. Place the clementines in the water and boil for 1 hour. Drain and let cool until cool enough to handle, about 10 minutes.

Preheat the oven to 350°F (180°C, or gas mark 4). Grease and line the bottom of a 9-inch (23-cm) springform pan with parchment paper.

Cut each clementine in half, remove the seeds, and discard them. Transfer the clementines, peel and all, to a food processor or blender and process until smooth.

In a large mixing bowl, combine the almond flour and baking powder. Whisk together. Add the eggs, sugar, clementine purée, vanilla, and melted butter and whisk until combined. Pour batter into pan.

Bake for 1 hour, or until a toothpick inserted into the center of the cake comes out clean.

Take the cake out of the oven and prick the cake all over with a toothpick. While the cake is still hot, pour the honey over the top of the cake and let it absorb fully into the cake, about 20 minutes.

Run a sharp knife along the edge of the pan, then unmold the cake and refrigerate until cold. Serve cold with whipped cream.

YIELD: 8 SERVINGS

Flourless Chocolate Cake with Hazelnuts

This cake is dense, moist, and super chocolaty. Perfect for entertaining, it can be made ahead and kept at room temperature for two days. Serve with freshly whipped cream or ice cream.

FOR CAKE:

¾ CUP (168 G) UNSALTED BUTTER, CUT INTO CUBES

1 BAG (12 OUNCES, OR 340 G) BITTER-SWEET CHOCOLATE CHIPS OR 12 OUNCES (340 G) CHOPPED BITTERSWEET CHOCOLATE

6 LARGE EGGS, SEPARATED

¾ CUP (150 G) SUGAR, DIVIDED

1 TABLESPOON (15 ML) VANILLA EXTRACT

¼ TEASPOON ALMOND EXTRACT

½ CUP (60 G) CHOPPED ROASTED HAZELNUTS

¼ TEASPOON SALT

FOR GLAZE:

½ CUP (120 ML) HEAVY CREAM

½ CUP (160 G) DARK CORN SYRUP

¾ CUP (130 G) DARK CHOCOLATE CHIPS

2 TABLESPOONS (30 ML) FRANGELICO HAZELNUT LIQUEUR

CHEF'S TIP *A small offset spatula can be used to coax the glaze over the edges of the cake and keep the surface smooth and even.*

To make the cake: Preheat the oven to 350°F (180°C, or gas mark 4). Grease a 9-inch (23-cm) springform pan. Line the bottom of pan with a circle of parchment paper, cut to fit, then grease the paper.

In a small saucepan over low heat, melt the butter and chocolate, stirring until smooth. Remove from heat and set aside.

Using an electric mixer, beat the egg yolks and half of the sugar (6 tablespoons [72 g]) in a large bowl until the mixture is very thick and pale, about 3 minutes. Stir the cooled chocolate mixture into the yolk mixture, then fold in the vanilla extract, almond extract, and hazelnuts.

Using clean dry beaters and a clean bowl, beat the egg whites and salt until soft peaks form. Gradually sprinkle in the remaining half of the sugar, beating as you go, until stiff peaks form. Fold half of the egg whites into the chocolate mixture to lighten the mixture, then gently fold in the remaining egg whites, taking care not to deflate the batter. Pour the batter into the prepared pan.

Bake until the top is puffed and cracked, about 45 minutes. Cool the cake in the pan on a rack (the cake will deflate).

To make the glaze: In a small saucepan, bring the cream and corn syrup to a low boil. Add the chocolate and whisk until smooth. Remove from the heat and stir in the Frangelico. Set aside.

Flatten down the top of the deflated cake with your fingers (the top will be crispy, and will crack and crumble a bit, so just push it into the cake gently). Run a sharp knife around the perimeter of the cake to loosen it. Unhinge and remove the rim of the springform pan. Carefully invert the cake onto your hand. Slide the cake back onto the base of the springform pan. Peel off the parchment paper.

Place the cake on a wire rack set over a counter lined with aluminum foil or parchment paper. Spread the glaze smoothly over the top and let it run down over the sides of the cake. Refrigerate until set, 20 minutes, then store the cake at room temperature.

YIELD: 10 SERVINGS

Pistachio and Apricot Macarons

I love walking into a fancy patisserie and seeing all of the different macarons in the case. I always choose a variety with pistachio, my favorite flavor. And despite what you may think, macarons are quite easy to make!

½ CUP (75 G) ROASTED SHELLED PISTACHIOS (MORE IF NEEDED), PLUS ADDITIONAL FINELY CHOPPED FOR GARNISH

1 CUP (120 G) POWDERED SUGAR

2 LARGE EGG WHITES, AT ROOM TEMPERATURE

¼ CUP (50 G) GRANULATED SUGAR

4-6 DROPS GREEN FOOD COLORING

½ CUP (160 G) APRICOT JAM

> **CHEF'S TIP** *It's tempting to want to eat or serve these right away after all of your hard work, but macarons won't achieve their perfectly soft and chewy consistency without "aging" for 24 hours in the fridge.*
>
> **VARIATION** *Fill these with any seedless jam you like, or even chocolate ganache or flavored buttercream.*

Preheat the oven to 300°F (150°C, or gas mark 2). Line 3 baking sheets with parchment paper and set aside.

Place the pistachios in a food processor and chop until very fine. Sift the mixture through a fine-mesh sieve, then place the coarse nut pieces that didn't pass through the sieve back into the food processor. Continue to process until all of the ground nuts pass through the sieve. Measure to make sure that you have exactly ¾ cup (75 g) pistachio flour. Sift the pistachio flour with the powdered sugar and set aside.

Place the egg whites and granulated sugar into the bowl of an electric mixer. Beat on high speed until soft peaks form. Continuing to beat, add the green food coloring, a few drops at a time, until you achieve the desired color green you would like your cookies to be, and the egg whites form stiff peaks.

Add the flour mixture to the egg whites and fold until the mixture has deflated and is smooth and shiny. You will know you have the right consistency when you scoop a dollop of the batter onto the batter in the bowl and within 20 seconds it has "melted" into the batter.

Transfer the batter to a pastry bag fitted with a ½-inch (1.3-cm) plain round tip, and pipe 1-inch (2.5-cm) rounds 1 inch (2.5 cm) apart onto the parchment-lined baking sheets. The rounds should look smooth and flat; if they have peaks, you have not folded your batter enough. (If this happens, squeeze the mixture back into the bowl, and beat a few more strokes. Make sure that a dollop of the batter "melts" into the batter after 20 seconds.) Pipe 48 circles onto the 3 baking sheets, then firmly tap each sheet onto the work surface 3 times to release any trapped air. If desired, sprinkle the macarons with the finely chopped pistachios for decoration.

(continued on next page)

(continued from previous page)

Let the piped batter stand at room temperature for 45 minutes; this will ensure your macarons bake properly. They should rise slightly and come out with a smooth top and a ruffled-looking bottom called the "foot".

Bake 1 sheet at a time for 18 minutes, rotating about halfway through cooking, until the macarons are crisp and easily release from the parchment when you pick them up.

Let the macarons cool directly on the baking sheets. Bake the remaining macarons in the same way. Once all of the cookies are cooked and cooled, sandwich 2 macarons with 1 teaspoon of the apricot preserves. Place the sandwiched cookies into an airtight container and refrigerate for 24 hours to soften before eating, then store at room temperature. If desired, the cookies may also be frozen for up to 3 months.

YIELD: 24 MACARONS

Five-Ingredient PB&J Cookies

I used to love making these cookies as a little girl! We always had the ingredients in the house, so if I had the urge to bake, these were a go-to treat. Anyone can make these, and everyone enjoys them!

2   **CUPS (520 G) CREAMY PEANUT BUTTER**

1½   **CUPS (340 G) PACKED LIGHT BROWN SUGAR**

2   **EGGS**

1   **TABLESPOON (15 ML) VANILLA EXTRACT**

½   **CUP (160 G) STRAWBERRY JELLY**

+ VARIATIONS
- *Peanut allergy? Try making these with creamy almond butter instead!*
- *Skip the jelly, bake the cookies plain, then while they are still hot, press either a mini peanut butter cup or a chocolate kiss into the center of each cookie.*

Preheat the oven to 350°F (180°C, or gas mark 4). Grease 2 cookie sheets and set aside.

In the bowl of a stand mixer, combine the peanut butter, brown sugar, eggs, and vanilla. Beat on medium speed until smooth and creamy, about 1 minute.

Drop by tablespoonfuls onto the greased cookie sheets, about ½ inch (1.3 cm) apart. Use your thumb to make an impression in the center of each cookie, then spoon a bit of the strawberry jelly into the impression in each cookie.

Bake for 7 to 9 minutes, or until the cookies just start to set and are golden brown on the bottom. Let the cookies cool for 3 to 4 minutes on the cookie sheets before using a spatula to carefully transfer the cookies to a cooling rack.

Once the cookies are completely cooled, store in an airtight container.

YIELD: 24 COOKIES

Penuche Fudge

Penuche fudge is a delicious vanilla fudge flavored with maple and brown sugar. It's heavenly as is, but is even better with a variety of delicious toppings. See below for some great variations.

2   CANS (5 OUNCES, OR 150 ML EACH) EVAPORATED MILK

2½ CUPS (575 G) PACKED LIGHT BROWN SUGAR

½   CUP (120 ML) MAPLE SYRUP

1   CUP (225 G) UNSALTED BUTTER

¾   TEASPOON SALT

1   CUP (120 G) POWDERED SUGAR

1   TABLESPOON (15 ML) VANILLA EXTRACT

2½ CUPS (300 G) CHOPPED WALNUTS OR PECANS

CHEF'S TIP *Your fudge might look "broken" or lumpy when it's done cooking. Don't fear! Once you incorporate the powdered sugar, keep beating the mixture on high speed until it is smooth and creamy.*

Line two 5 x 9-inch (12.5 x 23-cm) loaf pans with a strip of parchment paper. Leave the paper long enough so that it hangs over two sides of the pans (this will make it easy to lift the fudge out of the pans once it cools). Spray the pans and parchment lightly with nonstick spray.

Combine the evaporated milk, brown sugar, maple syrup, butter, and salt in a large saucepan. Cook the mixture over medium-high heat, stirring occasionally, until it comes to a boil. Decrease the heat to medium, then cook for an additional 20 to 30 minutes, or until the mixture reaches 240°F (116°C) on a candy thermometer.

Carefully transfer the hot mixture to the bowl of an electric mixer. Add the powdered sugar and vanilla and beat on low for 1 to 2 minutes, until the mixture is combined. Once the powdered sugar is incorporated, turn the mixer to high and beat for about 10 minutes, until the fudge begins to cool and is very creamy. Fold in the nuts, then scrape into the prepared pans.

Refrigerate, uncovered, for about 30 minutes, or until completely set. Lift the fudge out of the pan using the parchment "handles." Cut each pan of fudge into 16 pieces. Store in an airtight container.

YIELD: 32 PIECES

+ VARIATION *Once you pour the fudge into the pans, top with marshmallows, coconut, chocolate bits, a swirl of peanut butter, or chunks of your favorite g-free candy bar. I like to make one pan plain and top the other!*

Dairy-Free Caramelized Peach Ice Cream

You will not miss the dairy in this creamy, smooth ice cream. This recipe can be used with other fruits as well (I love it with pineapple, too). Feel free to get creative!

1   VANILLA BEAN

3   CUPS (705 ML) WHOLE COCONUT MILK

    PINCH OF SALT

¾ CUP (150 G) GRANULATED SUGAR

1   TEASPOON COCONUT OIL OR TRANS-FAT-FREE MARGARINE

½ CUP (85 G) PEELED, DICED FRESH PEACHES

1   TABLESPOON (15 G) BROWN SUGAR

¼ TEASPOON GROUND CINNAMON

5   LARGE EGG YOLKS

1   TEASPOON VANILLA EXTRACT

> ✗ **CHEF'S TIP** *Make this a traditional dairy ice cream by substituting 2 cups (470 ml) cream and 1 cup (235 ml) milk for the coconut milk. The method stays the same.*

Use a sharp knife to cut the vanilla bean in half lengthwise. Scrape the seeds out of the vanilla bean and place the seeds and the bean in a saucepan. Add the coconut milk, salt, and granulated sugar. Bring to a light simmer over medium heat, remove from the heat, and allow the mixture to steep for 1 hour.

Heat a skillet over medium heat, add the coconut oil, and heat to melt. Add the peaches and sauté until the peaches are lightly browned and the juices have reduced, about 5 minutes. Add the brown sugar and cinnamon, and cook for 2 to 3 more minutes, or until the brown sugar has melted. Let cool to room temperature, then refrigerate until ready to use.

Put the saucepan with the coconut milk back on the heat and reheat to warm. In the meantime, in a medium bowl, whisk the egg yolks. Slowly pour the warm milk into the yolks while whisking continuously. Pour the mixture back into the saucepan and cook over medium-low heat, stirring and scraping the bottom of the pan with a wooden spoon, until it begins to thicken. The custard is cooked when it is thick enough to coat the back of the spoon.

Strain the custard through a fine-mesh sieve into a large bowl. Stir in the vanilla extract and refrigerate until well chilled, several hours or preferably overnight.

Pour the custard into an ice cream maker and freeze according to the manufacturer's instructions. Swirl in the caramelized peaches, then place in a 1-quart (1-L) container, cover, and freeze until completely set, 3 to 4 hours.

◪ **YIELD: 1 QUART (1 L)**

Flambéed Bananas Foster

This dish is traditionally made tableside at restaurants, making great fanfare out of the flaming display, but it's simple to do at home. Sweet bananas are cooked in butter and brown sugar, finished with dark rum, and ignited into a rich and decadent topping for vanilla ice cream.

2   **CUPS (280 G) VANILLA ICE CREAM**

3   **TABLESPOONS (42 G) BUTTER**

¼   **CUP (60 G) PACKED BROWN SUGAR**

2   **LARGE, SLIGHTLY UNDER-RIPE BANANAS, PEELED AND SLICED INTO ½-INCH (6-MM)-THICK SLICES**

¼   **CUP (60 ML) DARK RUM**

     SPRINKLE OF GROUND CINNAMON

✗ CHEF'S TIP *Never pour alcohol directly from the bottle into a pan. The alcohol can ignite and the flames can jump into the bottle, making it very dangerous. Measure the alcohol out, then pour it into the pan.*

Spoon the ice cream into 4 bowls and place in the freezer until ready to serve.

In a large sauté pan over medium heat, melt the butter. Add the brown sugar, stir, and cook until melted, about 2 minutes. Add the banana slices and cook, stirring occasionally, until the edges of the bananas begin to soften and appear more rounded, about 3 minutes.

Remove the pan from the heat and carefully add the rum. If the pan is very hot, the alcohol may ignite on its own. If not, use a long-reach lighter to carefully ignite the rum. Shake the pan gently, until the flames go out. Sprinkle with the cinnamon and spoon over the bowls of ice cream.

▮ YIELD: 4 SERVINGS

Mango Margarita Sorbet

The perfect spiked summer dessert! I serve this in chilled margarita glasses rimmed with sugar.

½   **CUP (100 G) SUGAR**

4   **OR 5 (ABOUT 2½ POUNDS [1138 G]) RIPE MANGOES, PEELED, SEEDED, AND CUBED**

¼   **CUP (60 ML) TEQUILA**

¼   **CUP (60 ML) FRESH LIME JUICE**

    PINCH OF SALT

> **CHEF'S TIP** *I prefer the small paisley-shaped mangoes called Ataulfo mangoes. I find they have the best flavor and the creamiest consistency.*

Place the sugar, cubed mangoes, tequila, lime juice, and salt into a food processor and purée until smooth and the sugar has dissolved, 3 to 4 minutes. (Taste the purée, and if you can feel any sugar granules, continue to process until dissolved.)

Place in an ice cream maker. Freeze according to the manufacturer's instructions, then transfer to a 1-quart (1-L) container and freeze until completely set, 3 to 4 hours.

YIELD: 1 QUART (1 L)

ACKNOWLEDGMENTS

My deepest thanks to my literary agent, Marilyn Allen, for her guidance. Thanks to Amanda Waddell; my editor, Karen Levy; Heather Godin, Renae Haines, and the fantastic team at Fair Winds for their support on this project. To the wonderful photography team, Theresa Raffetto, Matthew Vohr, Corey Belle Earling, and Penelope Bouklas: thank you for bringing my recipes to life.

To Mark and Leigh Teixeira: I could have never done this without your incredibly generous support and patience. Thank you for believing in me and for letting me test endless recipes on your family. It's a privilege and an honor to work with you each day. To Allison Rutberg and Melina Bustamante: thanks for being my on-the-job cheerleaders and taste testers.

To Harry Figgie: thanks for being someone I can lean on and count on each day. To Gillian Menza, for believing I could do it right from the start. To Jennifer Siemon, the very best friend a girl could ask for and a talented chef: I can't thank you enough for your help with this project and for supporting me in so many ways To Jen and Uli Iserloh: thank you for your guidance and for all you've taught me. My thanks to Jessica Seinfeld, for my first glimpse into the cookbook world, and for all that I learned along the way.

Gratitude and love to my family for always believing in me, especially my mom Chris, stepdad Wayne, sister Rachel, brother Peter, and grandma Ginny. Lastly, a million thanks to my dad Gerard, for the hours and hours he spent with me at my dining room table doing research for this book. I would have been lost without your help; thank you.

ABOUT THE AUTHOR

Olivia Dupin is a private chef, recipe developer, and consultant. Since being diagnosed with celiac disease in 2009, she has been committed to creating simple, delicious, gluten-free recipes so that those with restrictions can still enjoy the foods they love.

Olivia is a graduate of the Culinary Institute of America and has worked as a private chef to clients such as professional baseball player Mark Teixeira of the New York Yankees and comedian and television star Jerry Seinfeld. She is also a consultant and recipe developer for Energy Kitchen Restaurants, a healthy restaurant franchise.

Olivia maintains a recipe blog for Energy Kitchen at www.energykitchen.com, as well as her own blog dedicated to simple, home-style, gluten-free recipes at www.livglutenfree.com. She lives, cooks, and writes in Jersey City, New Jersey.

INDEX